16 50

D0871182

GREGORY

J

GILLESPIE

By

ABRAM LERNER

Director

Hirshhorn Museum and Sculpture Garden

HIRSHHORN MUSEUM AND SCULPTURE GARDEN

SMITHSONIAN INSTITUTION

Published by

Smithsonian Institution Press

City of Washington

1977

Exhibition Dates:

Hirshhorn Museum and Sculpture Garden
December 22, 1977-February 12, 1978

Georgia Museum of Art
The University of Georgia, Athens
April 23-May 14, 1978

Photographic Credits   Raffaele Baldi: pp. 39, 54
Geoffrey Clements: pp. 58, 74
eeva-inkeri: pp. 46, 55, 63, 69, 93, 96, 98, 100
Thomas Feist: pp. 75, 81, 94
Walter Rosenblum: pp. 36, 40
Walter Russell: pp. 59, 95, 99
John Tennant: pp. 32, 33, 34, 37, 51, 52
Jann & John Thomson: p. 76

Cover: Detail. *Self-Portrait in Studio*, 1976-77
(catalogue number 73).

Library of Congress Cataloging in Publication Data
Main entry under title:

Gregory Gillespie.

Based on an exhibition held at the Hirshhorn Museum
and Sculpture Garden, Dec. 22, 1977-Feb. 12, 1978.
Bibliography: p.
Includes index.
1. Gillespie, Gregory. I. Lerner, Abram.
II. Hirshhorn Museum and Sculpture Garden.
ND237.G447L47   759.13   77-16158

Paperback edition
For sale by the Superintendent of Documents
United States Government Printing Office
Washington, D.C. 20402
Stock number 047-003-00056-3

Printing by Rapoport Printing Corp.

Contents

Dr. and Mrs. H. A. T. Bailey, Jr., Little Rock, Arkansas
Mrs. George Boynton, Tuxedo Park, New York
Jane Calvin, Santa Monica, California
Mr. and Mrs. Daniel W. Dietrich II, Chester Springs, Pennsylvania
Joseph Feury and Lee Grant, Malibu Beach, California
Dr. and Mrs. Sidney Fierst, Brooklyn, New York
Bella and Sol Fishko, New York
Joseph and Deirdre Garton, Madison, Wisconsin
George Gilbert, New York
William A. Gumberts, Evansville, Indiana
Graham Gund, Cambridge, Massachusetts
Joseph H. Hirshhorn, Washington, D.C.
Mr. and Mrs. Philip Horowitz, Long Island City, New York
Mr. and Mrs. Jacob M. Kaplan, New York
Robert and Beverly Katz, Rome
Mr. and Mrs. John Koch, New York
Sydney and Frances Lewis, Richmond, Virginia
Alfred Ordover, New York
Mr. and Mrs. Peter B. Ornstein, New York
Mr. and Mrs. Stephen D. Paine, Boston
Jerome Reich, Boston
Mr. and Mrs. James M. Sampson, Hingham, Massachusetts
Ira Schwartz, New York
Helen Searing, Northampton, Massachusetts
Daniel Selznick, Los Angeles
Rheta Sosland, Shawnee Mission, Kansas
Allan Stone, New York
Janet Thomas Swanson, Cutchogue, New York
Mr. and Mrs. John Wasserman, New York
Mr. and Mrs. Charles K. Wilmers, Geneva
Nathaniel Zimskind
Anonymous collectors

Forum Gallery, New York
Georgia Museum of Art, The University of Georgia, Athens
Nebraska Art Association, Thomas C. Woods Memorial Collection, Lincoln
Museum of Art, The Pennsylvania State University, University Park
Sara Roby Foundation Collection, New York
Creative Arts Center, West Virginia University, Morgantown
Whitney Museum of American Art, New York

Acknowledgments

In the spirit of first things first, I would like to express my warm thanks to Gregory Gillespie for his cooperation during the planning stages of this exhibition. Without his help there obviously could have been no exhibition. On every occasion, he met our requests for information with patience and candor, in a spirit of participation which made our association particularly agreeable. This was especially true of his willingness to be interviewed for publication in this catalogue. It required that he sacrifice many hours of his valuable time to undergo the rigors of cross-examination. For this he has my special thanks.

Bella Fishko, Director of the Forum Gallery, earns our particular thanks for her consistently helpful attitude. Her deep faith in Gillespie, whom she has represented since 1964, and her familiarity with all aspects of his work, made her assistance essential. Always eager to lighten our task, she and her assistant, Lili Gross, were generous with their time and responsive to our unending queries. In helping us to locate and reach the many owners of Gillespie's paintings, as well as making available to us photographs and other records of the artist's career, and for much more, I extend my deep appreciation.

It is a special pleasure to thank the many lenders who so generously agreed to part, even temporarily, with their treasures so that we could make this the most complete presentation of Gillespie's work to date. Their cooperation was of paramount importance and I have rarely seen such a willing and warm response to our loan requests. I trust their generosity will be repaid by the pleasure they will take in this exhibition.

In particular, I want to thank Howard Fox of the Museum's Department of Painting and Sculpture, who spent long hours in diligent pursuit of everything relating to our project. His researches have given this publication whatever scholarly attributes it has. His enthusiasm and perception were outstanding factors in helping me bring this catalogue and exhibition to fruition. To have accomplished this with grace and good humor as well, made his assistance all the more gratifying.

Barbara Butts, a summer Museum intern in 1976, was instrumental in completing preliminary research on Gillespie's career, and her successor this year, Kimerly Rorschach, has assisted in updating the bibliography. I thank them heartily.

Finally, I want to express my gratitude to Stephen Kraft of the Smithsonian Institution Press, who has once again been a most patient and helpful collaborator in guiding us through the ordeals and delights of publication.

A.L.

Introduction

ABRAM LERNER We can conceive of Gillespie's paintings as private interior landscapes into which we are transported by the power of the artist's imagination and the cunning of his hand. We become travelers in a strange and fascinating region where we may experience the metamorphosis of places, objects, and people, and where the simplest things, painted with painstaking clarity, become bewitched and transformed. Gillespie has the power to excite in us sensations which are rare in contemporary figurative art, by reaching through the veil of the subject to its essential nature and force. He is a romantic with gothic affinities, a realist who is also a Surrealist, a visionary and a moralist in whose art the sentiment and unease of our time are merged. One might speak of Gillespie as a social critic were his art less circuitous and subjective. One cannot find specific references to social conditions in his paintings, only indirect references to the human condition. We can interpret his iconography without ever really being certain of his intention. In fact, we are faced with the most precisely painted subjects whose meaning remains mysteriously uncertain.

For many young artists in the fifties and sixties, Italy was not only a haven where they could work peacefully, undeterred by the clamor of opposing theories and styles, it was an ambience where certain spirits could soar, where the great art of the past was a living presence encountered on every piazza, yet where contemporary Italian society formed a mosaic of the most vivid and unique diversity which could be readily observed and cherished by the foreigner.

The effect of Italy on Gillespie's work is explicit; it entered his life in subtle ways and was visually expressed in his choice of Italian subjects. He mentions Masaccio and Carlo Crivelli as among his favorites, and indeed we can observe the strong influence of Italian art as well as contemporary Italian life in his early paintings. Direct influences do not persist, however, and it is the feel and mood of Italian painting which we sense rather than direct references to particular masters. Indeed, there may be a greater empathy between his essentially romantic sensibility and the German and Flemish masters. This is noticeable in those early works in which the sharpness of physical detail and the dramatic emphasis have more in common with Grünewald, Bruegel, and Bosch than with their more gracious and elegant Italian counterparts. The experience of Renaissance humanism expressed through religious iconography had a liberating effect on Gillespie, stimulating him to create paintings which are in effect aimed against religious orthodoxy, yet contain repeated allusions to his deep yearning for some mode of faith and purification.

In the matter of technique, Gillespie is similarly indebted to Italian art. This is seen in his use of wooden panels, which he prefers to canvas because of their resistant surface and greater strength; his love of gesso for its smooth surface and malleability, the thin layers of paint glazed or applied with a fine sable brush and brought to an adamantine finish; and his use of the Renaissance perspective grid. In contrast, his introduction of photocollage and even nonart material constitutes a modernization of his technical means.

But it was essentially the contemporary Italian scene which affected him most deeply. The Roman trattorias and interiors take on the quality of stage sets in which sad and disquieting dramas will be enacted. Occasionally, as if from some claustrophobic need, a tiny window allows us a glimpse of a city, some architectural monument perhaps; or a niche and a few photographs enliven a somber wall. These are hardly tourist views of sunny Italy; they have more in common with the films of De Sica and Fellini in their sober and often tragic articulation of contemporary Italian life. Like the films of those masters of cinema, Gillespie's subjects reflect the traumas and anxieties of our time. His work abounds in disturbing variations of reality which mirror our normal experiences but transform what is hauntingly familiar into an alarming blend of hallucination and sharp observation. Nothing is as it seems; alterations and mutations challenge our perceptual equilibrium and our sense of certainty. Each painting is a kind of theater in which objects or characters act out ambiguous dramas, their roles reversed, redefined, or shifted.

In a seemingly straightforward painting such as *Landscape at Night,* 1962-63 (cat. no. 4), we are vaguely disturbed by the reclining nude figure. Is she a recumbent mythological fiction or a victim of some violent malefaction? Is the wall behind her intended to hide the deed or is it simply a pictorial device? Another early painting, *Allegorical Street Scene,* completed in 1963 (cat. no. 1), depicts a thoroughfare with spectators, passersby, and the facade of a house. While the woman holding the child recalls the Masaccio *Eve* in the Brancacci Chapel in the way the figure strides and her head is tilted, there is no avenging angel, only a mutilated, androgynous figure who looks on passively, momentarily distracted. A rather stylish young woman (who repeats the mother's pose in reverse) and an oddly immobilized couple idly look on. The figures share no common purpose, yet they seem related in some way, and it is hardly likely that this painting, which is technically handled with such deliberate innocence, should achieve such a disconcerting effect by mere chance.

Gillespie places great emphasis on the direct use of photographs in his earlier work. Given his fascination with the more bizarre aspects of society, he discovered a source of endless material in the newspaper and magazine photographs which serve as our mirrors onto the world. Sorting and clipping those photographs which struck a response, he explored new relationships and affinities between them. Responding to their suggestive power, he reconciled images which had no common origin, arranging his collages into pictorial compositions from which various themes emerged. Having thus created the basic foundation of his composition, he painted over the entire surface, frequently disguising his source by transforming individual elements, eliminating others, or adding to the whole. In this fashion, beginning with disparate photo fragments, he was able to create a unified work which heightened those incongruous and psychological images which had originally sparked his interest. Gillespie's use of photographs must be considered a primary factor in his development. It acted both as source and stimulus and enlarged his technical capability, enabling him to impart a greater degree of verisimilitude to his paintings, a quality essential to sustain the viewer's acceptance of his imagery. In the past few years, he has made far less use of the collage technique, painting directly from nature and only on occasion using photographs as reference sources.

One of the earliest paintings in the exhibition, *Two Men Seated,* 1961-62 (cat. no. 2), shows an interior with two middle-aged men. The figures are illuminated, but they exist in semidarkness. Their pose is relaxed and they might very well be patients in a waiting room. Yet we are conscious of an unexplained tension filling the room. Is it something that has just been said, some unpleasant gesture or remark that has offended or startled? We are filled with curiosity, as if we had chanced on the scene and were waiting impatiently for the tension to be resolved. To persuade us and bring our interest forward to such a degree, it is necessary that the painting be so convincing that we are not aware of the means used to achieve this end. In much modern art, our pleasure arises from an opposite source: we delight in the process itself, in following the artist's progress through the brushmarks, stains, and other evidence of the act of painting which constitute the structure and skin of the work. In Gillespie's paintings, as in those of the masters whom he admires, the method or technique is almost incidental, at least until we have first sensed the picture's substance and imagery. It is not unlike listening to a musical performance in which the music is so compelling that we are nearly unaware of the performer's skill.

Throughout the early work one is conscious of human estrangement and isolation as a constant and brooding presence. Gillespie's universe is filled with strange and sparkling detail, with small groups of forlorn figures in a city square or in intimate landscapes which remind us of those precious Gothic fancies in which every tree and hill represents all of the known world. People seem unaware of each other's presence, or accept it tranquilly as a source of self-indulgent diversion. One senses their indifference to the exploitation of other human beings. Bathers pursue their lonely ablutions, people walk out of scenes in dispirited isolation, individuals are portrayed in cramped spaces staring dejectedly or walking without apparent purpose across empty rooms and lonely streets. Where relationships are evident, they seem to result in further and greater unhappiness, even brutality. In the Whitney Museum's *Two Women,* 1965 (cat. no. 13), we intrude on a domestic scene and encounter two women, one nude, the other clothed. The nude figure stares out at us, dejected yet defiant. Her nudity is palpably vulnerable and her pose suggests a surrender, an acceptance of some inevitable circumstance. The linearity of the figure and the full light which rakes it mercilessly add a pathos to the scene which is heightened by the presence of another and older figure in a robe, who stands with hands clasped in the shallow, shadowed space of the room, her face only dimly visible. What is their relationship and why does it make us uneasy? The title doesn't help, and we are left to our own speculations. Gillespie offers no solutions to these narrative puzzles. Aside from explaining his working method and his need to paint accurately what he observes, he says only that when his subject chooses to go off in strange directions, he offers no resistance.

In turning away from the popular aesthetic of the sixties, Gillespie reduced the physical scale of his paintings, in sharp contrast to the enormous canvases then being produced. The small format may have resulted from his working method, that is, the use of photographs and magazine clippings, but their effect is intense, demanding close and careful scrutiny, promising some rare insight or secret to the sensitive observer. Small paintings share in this power when their quality is high; one thinks of Simone Martini, Clouet, certain delicious, small, Cubist Picassos, and so forth. It should be noted that in his late works Gillespie's panels have greatly expanded in size, suggesting that the small scale was never a contraction of larger designs or concepts, but a necessary and final format, determined by his expressive needs at the time.

Beginning in 1967 with such paintings as *Untitled Portrait (Man Enshrined)* (not in exhibition), *Three Sisters,* 1969 (cat. no. 31), and *Woman on Blue Ground,* 1969 (cat. no. 30), strong currents of sexual references, explicit or insinuated, dominate Gillespie's paintings. The most innocent objects become endowed with phallic or visceral properties, even still lifes and interiors. In the complexities of a wall recess, the details of a plant form or the contours of a squash, a special or erotic element is either specifically noted or illusionistically implied. On occasion, these references are carried to extremes in morbid sexual fantasies where brutality, amputation, and seduction are components in sad and mortifying rituals. Unhappiness and pity permeate some of the more specific paintings in which people are depicted as brutalized, injured, or debased. In *Seated Man and Girl,* 1965-67 (cat. no. 14), one is struck by a persistent sense of isolation in a scene which, on the contrary, should suggest intimacy. The situation appears promising for only one participant in this odd confrontation in which two people, perhaps strangers, are bound together in an illicit and pathetic relationship. There is certainly no sense of pleasure or rapture suggested in any of these paintings and one may conjecture that they are reflections of a particular crisis in the artist's personal life.

The *Imaginary Self-Portrait,* 1963 (cat. no. 5), began a series of portraits which recorded the artist's self-perception as well as the evolution of his expressive means. This 1963 portrait is traditional in design; one is tempted to compare it to certain Renaissance portraits (Antonella da Messina comes to mind) with its frontal pose, compressed space, and compelling gaze. The emphasis is on the face, especially on the eyes, which draw our attention despite the activity glimpsed through the window. The figure is set in shallow space, relieved by the implied depth of the window ledge opening onto a narrow vertical aperture which looks out on a street where the curb defines the space as if it were a double cinema screen. A hypnotic stare and intense introspection constitute the dominant mood of succeeding self-portraits. In *Self-Portrait in Black Shirt,* 1968-69 (cat. no. 28), Gillespie acknowledges his real identity. The subject is center stage, the color considerably heightened and the sense of seclusion more pronounced. In front of a flatly painted green wall delineated by variations of the same color, the figure is placed squarely; the head is dominant and almost ferocious in its expression, the eyes focusing on some inner vision. The drawing is more linear, the body outlined and encased in a tight shirt which literally forces the skin to crease and swell. The portrait is in the nature of a confrontation, the artist defiantly declaring his presence and independence. Strangely primitive in its manner and effect, the painting explores the face in great detail and sets the stage for even more minute investigation in future portraits. It is interesting to compare this painting with *Self-Portrait (Foro Romano),* 1969 (cat. no. 36), in which Gillespie identifies himself more directly with his art and where his self-portrait is only a detail in the total painting. No longer in isolation, the artist confronts his visionary universe and the real world. The collaged postcard of Rome tells us where he is, the painting in its entirety what he is, and the self-portrait, a photocollage, establishes the artist's presence within the contradictory impulses which generate his art. In contrast to the writhing organisms which emerge from the blood-red wall as from some disembowled creature, compelling because they are so very human, the artist looks out with detached intensity, while the blue sky of Rome reveals its familiar ruins and its ancient seal mingles past and present.

In *Self-Portrait (Bald),* 1971-72 (cat. no. 47), the head and shoulders once more dominate the painting. Light falls on the forehead and upper part of the face, the background is neutral and loosely brushed. The strong modeling of the head is emphasized by the drawing, which outlines the figure in space and conveys the solidity of the forms. The face seems pensive if not tranquil, its expression withdrawn and contemplative, in marked contrast to the challenging posture of the earlier (1968-69) portrait in black shirt. The eyes look past us, the shaved head, which is tilted in an attitude of absorbed attention, is dramatized by the strong contrast of light and dark which adds emphasis to what might be the study of a penitent. Clearly in the same contemplative mood, the large *Self-Portrait on Bed,* 1973-74 (cat. no. 64), locates the artist in an interior which suggests a cell. Seated on a low mattress, the artist crouches listlessly, staring past the observer, arms resting loosely on his thighs, legs slack. We are immediately drawn into the painting by the artist's intense and melancholy gaze, which pierces the picture space and rivets our attention. The figure is the single element in the painting which has been carefully modeled in strong relief; the rest is rendered in linear fashion, its depth implied by perspective drawing. The light is evenly diffused and illuminates the composition sharply. On a window ledge a pristine pear sits, the door to an adjoining room is ajar, a cabinet drawer is open, and an artist's palette appears in the foreground. We might be in the artist's studio and he could be looking past us toward a work in progress. But the intense introspection of his gaze suggests something beyond casual preoccupation. The limited space, the half-open door which could signify uncertainty or suspense, the bare mattress, all produce a solemn and resigned mood. Yet there is an air of expectancy, as if someone or something might suddenly arrive. Our eye is caught by the tiny figure of a kneeling, nude boy on the crossbar of a shelved niche. Its size and classic pose mark its remoteness, yet its presence suggests a conjurer's trick signifying some unusual event or prophecy. What connection can it have with the brooding figure on the bed except that it may offer us a link to the thoughts that engross him?

In *Self-Portrait (Torso)*, 1975 (cat. no. 66), the artist returns to a more direct confrontation. In this quarter-length figure, he once again focuses his unflinching gaze on us. The portrait is startling in its realism, in its sheer skill in rendering the details of flesh and body. This is enhanced by the subject's appearance—the long hair and beard and the naked torso might well belong to a Renaissance saint or holy man. For all its self-absorption and detachment, the portrait disturbs us by its tactility and physical presence, by its interchangeable lucidity and mystery. In an accompanying *Self-Portrait II*, 1976-77 (cat. no. 72), a half-length painting which at this writing is unfinished, the figure is placed slightly left of center, the face and body turned somewhat. The eyes still stare into our own, yet they look inward as well. One cannot fail to note the growing self-involvement in the character of these self-portraits. It becomes increasingly evident as Gillespie's skill grows in rendering the myriad details of observed facts. The pose which previously expressed anger, disdain, or challenge is now directed toward a more intense and detailed study of his appearance, without attaching to it any overt attitude.

The self-portrait continues to absorb him. It has helped him to arrive at the central core of his art, the convergence of appearance and reality. These images, with their strata of illusion and conception, their prodigious pictorial detail and intellectual synthesis, are works of the most personal and subjective nature. A self-portrait on which the artist is currently at work, *Self-Portrait in Studio* (cat. no. 73), shows him seated in his studio, looking out at us once more with that steadfast but veiled gaze. Judging it only from its unfinished state, this painting promises to be the most complex of his self-portraits, worked in minute detail and evolving what seems to be the most comprehensive view of himself to date. Psychologically, the portraits reveal a transition from a state of intense inner strife to a tranquil self-contemplation, an autobiographical account of the artist's shifting attitude toward himself and the world. Gillespie says of these paintings, "the last portraits are becoming more serene in a way, much less pain and suffering." In the formal sense, we discern a flowering of technical skill and an independence of pictorial means; a greater freedom from the influence of classical art; a growing reliance on direct observation; and a less elaborate, less self-conscious compositional structure.

An interesting aspect of Gillespie's work is its thematic continuity and his recurring use of motifs as elements of contrast, innovation, and renewal. He will frequently refer to an existing work within a new work. An example of this is *Woman in Brassiere,* 1965 (cat. no. 12), in which the striding figure in the background is the same as that in *Woman Walking in a Room,* 1965 (cat. no. 11). In the latter, she moves at random across a nearly empty room while in *Woman in Brassiere,* the same figure makes her appearance in the act of leaving the amorphous space which serves as the background for the major figure of the woman whose body is tightly constrained in a viselike garment. The inclusion of the figure from *Woman Walking in a Room,* who moves freely in her unrestricted nudity, almost floating out of the painting, makes a pointed contrast to the static and cruelly trussed figure of the *Woman in Brassiere.* Aside from such partial use of older paintings, Gillespie frequently introduces them in toto into new works. One can recognize specific self-portraits, still lifes, and other paintings in later works. In these transplantings Gillespie is effecting a continuity of theme and purpose. He is also implying that there is no clear distinction between art and experience; that he is in fact the subject, the interpreter, the spectator, and the immutable witness.

Toward the end of his stay in Italy, Gillespie produced several "shrine" paintings in which the subject is a section or corner of an ordinary room converted into a private but undefined reliquary. In *Bread Shrine* (cat. no. 32), a mixed-media painting done in 1969 and recently repainted, the artist creates a strong composition in sharp contrasts of horizontals and verticals, the colors raw and unyielding. A boldly painted tile pattern forms the background wall which supports a large block. An old-fashioned flower holder shaped in the form of a hand is (perplexingly) filled with fruit. On the face of the block, which is outlined with metal strips, is pointed a horizontal diamond shape in which are represented two loaves of bread and the risen Christ. In an opening in the tile wall below the block we find a group of very small figures occupied in some bizarre activity. Another opening discloses a view of a similar miniature purgatory. A window at the upper left looks out into a Roman piazza with figures. On the wall above the block hangs a print of a religious subject, and directly above it is a small version of another Gillespie work, *Woman with Baby (Crying),* 1968 (cat. no. 26). The total painting is a mixed metaphor containing references to religious myth, human suffering, and the mysteries which are revealed when we penetrate the orderly surface of things. Gillespie's reference to his own painting, whose subject might also be interpreted as a weeping Madonna and Child, strengthens the mood of revelation and pain: the harsh interior with its peeling wall and repetitive design, the optical dissonance of the floor pattern, the nostalgic Victorian vase, the creatures struggling in their catacombs behind the wall, and, finally, the view out on a grim, contemporary city square. This variety of themes is paralleled by the variety of materials used in representing them — metal strips, nails, plaster, wood, photographs, and so forth.

A related painting, *Naples Shrine,* 1969 (cat. no. 33), suggests an archeological discovery. An opening in a scarred wall reveals a complex checkerboard tile ledge which creates its own sharp perspective leading into a room beyond. The tiles and an upper window are rendered with compulsive detail, adding a *trompe l'oeil* quality to the foreground, while the interior beyond is only suggested by lightly drawn lines which give it a contrasting hallucinatory ambience. The object which occupies the center of this "shrine" appears in an opening on the far interior wall, a nude female torso. Again, one is confronted with the antipodes of illusion and reality, which converge in the secret chamber of our inner eye.

On his return to the United States there was no sudden change in Gillespie's work. In *Pumice Box and Orange Meditation Piece,* 1971 (cat. no. 46), which repeats the wall and niche theme of the "shrine" paintings, the artist retains the clashing reds and greens, the strongly patterned tiles, and the peeling wall. There is no central icon, but a strange, small figure sits astride a funnel-shaped object, and a drawing of a child appears on the niche wall. A cheese, an orange, and a checkerboard-design drinking cup are arranged on a ledge. The mixture of the real and the visionary here becomes titillating rather than unsettling, and though some areas of this otherwise carefully rendered painting are sketchy and fugitive (note the tubular element which is convincingly modeled below the upper shelf and merely indicated in line as it continues up through the shelf), it is a device the artist has employed in previous paintings.

In *The Hall Corner: Graves House,* 1971 (cat. no. 44), a door opens on a view outdoors which still bears a strong affinity to Gillespie's Italian landscapes, but the major emphasis is focused on the corner of the room in which the light, the reflected shadows, and the girl-scout photograph with its American flag all seem eminently familiar and homey. From that same year, *Northampton Motor Vehicle Department* (cat. no. 40) returns us to the Surrealist mood of the earlier work and transforms an innocently titled subject into a dream sequence in which once again a sense of isolation and alienation hovers over an everyday scene.

One of the most disturbing paintings done since Gillespie's return is *Hospital,* 1971 (cat. no. 41), which shows us three nurses performing some grisly task in a hospital laboratory. The nurses, happily engaged, smiling and obviously pleased, are up to their waists in cadavers, weird disemboweled creatures, and other frightening anatomical residue. The contrast is shattering, in part because the painting has the reality of a snapshot and the ring of truth. Its shock lies in its power to convince us that it *is* an image of truth rather than fantasy, that this nightmare may be more real than we dare think.

Two very skillful paintings of 1972 and 1973 illuminate an intimate world of distinctly American flavor: *Back Entrance: Post and Stone* (cat. no. 50) and *Under the Porch* (cat. no. 51). Here, in almost microscopic detail, are the odds and ends of the backyard—the hidden and neglected corners where the planks rot, the stones endure, and the weeds push their ragged way up through the littered and inhospitable soil. One can feel the damp gathered in shadowed recesses. Both paintings are designed with an admirable sensitivity to abstracted and simplified forms and textures. Rich detail is contrasted with a large spatial design, flecked surfaces with flat, expansive color areas.

Bosch-like fantasy reappears in such paintings as *Snake Painting,* 1973 (cat. no. 60), which returns to the open-wall theme, *Night Vegetation* (cat. no. 58), and *Night Garden* (cat. no. 59), also painted in 1973, in which spectral bodies multiply and renew themselves in eerie transformation. In marked contrast, *The Wedding,* 1972-73 (cat. no. 54), and *Double Portrait (Fran and Myself),* 1973 (cat. no. 55), which are based on photographs but were painted directly, come closest to Photorealism, a style which seems to have only minimal interest for Gillespie, whose use of photographs eschews imitation of their surface texture and effects. He prefers to transform the photographic image either by working directly on it, altering or eliminating as he chooses, or by transferring elements of the photographic image in the process as if he were painting from the model. The latter is the method used in these two paintings.

In 1973 Gillespie created a wall painting titled *Bonnie* (not in exhibition), which deals with the subject in a new way. Although the wall is still cracked, peeling, and nakedly autobiographical, it no longer yields scenes from a hidden interior. The subjects originate in the artist's immediate environment—paintings, photographs, toys, and other personal possessions. The open wounds, the revealing apertures with their secret inhabitants are gone. This painting is related to Gillespie's later and most ambitious wall painting of 1976.

In *Red Squash*, 1975 (cat. no. 68), the "shrine" theme reappears, this time without the disturbing quality of such previous paintings, a reminder of which is seen in the inclusion of an image of his own *Bread Shrine* (cat. no. 32) tacked to the wall. Nevertheless, this red squash is hardly a vegetable which can be viewed with equanimity. Its voluptuousness and its association with·a shrine could well make it appear an object of worship or a symbol of fertility luxuriating on a pagan alter. In *Still Life with Squash and Rutabagas,* 1975 (cat. no. 69), the vegetables take on anthropomorphic sexual characteristics. Unyielding, disdainful, and unnaturally alive, they form an uneasy alliance with an ordinary cardboard box. As in most of Gillespie's art, an air of ambiguity prevails. This is one of the strongest of the artist's recent paintings—in the handling of the powerful design, in the palpable essence of each object, and in the sense of reality which permeates its interior.

In *Studio Wall,* 1976 (cat. no. 70), the largest of his recent paintings, Gillespie mingles fragments of his art and life. Objects related only by their association with his work and family—masks, paintings, plants, vegetables, toys—all dominated by a studio manikin—are arranged against a wall. Some of the objects are rendered in *trompe l'oeil* fashion, others are painted in a straightfor-ward, nonillusionistic style. This mixture of conventional realism and outright illusion keeps the viewer's perceptions in a state of imbalance; the viewer's eye, deliberately stopped by jeweled areas of precise notation, leaps forward in sudden discovery of what appears to be a collage object, only to discover the error and return to painted areas whose figurations never penetrate the surface skin of the work. There is no straining for dazzling perspective or for the polished finish of a Harnett, yet the individual forms are convincingly defined and occupy their own space without destroying the flatness of the picture plane. Although the painting is not as detailed or finished as some others, an effect resulting in part from its size, the arrangement of shapes and patterns of color has been carefully planned without making the abstract nature of these decisions too obvious. Illusion, the depth or tactility of objects, is handled with a sparseness which has the virtue of creating a continuum of spatial perception. In keeping with its size, one cannot help but note a change, if not a departure, from Gillespie's psychologically imbued themes and variations; the niche, the commanding icon, the shallow rooms, the secret altar, and the erupting walls are present to some degree, but only as the subjects of the artist. An air of liberation permeates this autobiographical painting. The dark curtain, previously drawn aside to reveal only fragments of the artist's inner conflicts and dark imagination, is here lifted to disclose the dramatis personae of his creative life.

The current tendency to describe contemporary art in the cool, expository language demanded by abstractionist aesthetics makes it difficult to deal with an artist like Gillespie, whose paintings are in turn dramatic, nightmarish, metaphorical, and fleshed with real or implied psychological substance. In Gillespie's art, the pictorial architecture, which he constructs with great care, is in the end only a skeleton for a full body of literary and metaphysical references. One cannot do critical justice to Gillespie without involving oneself in subjective and emotive syntax. While it may help to know the Masters to better grasp Gillespie's means, it is equally important to have some understanding of the psychological imperatives that determine his content. We may divine Masaccio and Crivelli in some of these works, but the Cubists, Surrealists, Neo-Realists, Victorian Romanticists, and Sigmund Freud are equally present.

Gillespie's art embraces past and present with vitality and urgency; he reengages tradition in contemporary terms and offers us an opportunity to reconsider our aesthetic options. Gillespie's work is perhaps too personal and eccentric to create a school or to effect a shift in taste, but it has the persistent power of revelation. In his imagery and depiction of our contemporary *angst* Gillespie has few equals. There is nothing ingratiating about his art; it deals with secret yearnings and startling confrontations. His skill is formidable, yet he restrains it so that it may serve a larger purpose. Few artists have been as bold in renouncing the formulas of current fashion or have fought so zealously to recapture the drama of the subject in art. Fewer still have been able to pierce the facade of contemporary life and delineate its concurrent beauty and terror so profoundly.

An Interview with Gregory Gillespie

*(Gregory Gillespie was interviewed by
Abram Lerner and Howard Fox
at the Hirshhorn Museum and Sculpture
Garden in two sessions on March 24, 1977.
The following remarks are taken from
those sessions.)*

Q: *Your stay in Europe was made possible by a Fulbright-Hays Grant, am I correct?*

A: Yes, in part. The Fulbright was to study in Florence for one year, and was renewed for a second year. That was in 1962 and 1963. And then I got a Chester Dale Grant to study at the American Academy in Rome for the next three years.

Q: *Did you find any substantial difference between Florence and Rome?*

A: Yes. In Florence we lived in the country; that's while I was doing landscapes, and we were really out of the city, on the road to Bologna, about ten miles out of Florence, right *in* the landscape. I painted the landscapes and the people in them and a few of the street scenes — like the piazza scenes. But in Rome, at the American Academy, we were in the city. And I was more excited by the trattorias and restaurants and the interiors and the walls — the city aspects.

Q: *Then, where you were living had a great deal to do with what you were painting. This was the first time you had been to Italy; how were you affected by seeing the old masters for the first time?*

A: It was fantastic! We spent all our time in the Uffizzi. I went to art school in New York City — there was the Met. Or the Frick. But I wasn't really ready for them. After working in Italy for a few years, I started to become technically competent enough so that the impact of how they made things so real, with such volume and such dimension, was something I could begin to relate my own work to — as a goal.

Q: *Did you know the Masaccios in Florence?*

A: Of course. In fact, that was my project for the Fulbright, to study Masaccio.

Q: *Do you feel your work relates to his painting?*

A: You know his images, like the beggar and the woman holding the baby and the others — that was the kind of thing I was doing then, of people in the landscapes and in the streets. Some of the allegories I painted at that time attempted to deal with themes and subject matter as a kind of narrative, as Masaccio and a lot of other early Renaissance painters had done.

Q: *It's interesting because you were continuing a tradition which had religious origins. I suspect that what appealed to the later Renaissance artists was Masaccio's sophistication in humanizing his religious subject, his realism. Well then, you worked in Florence and then you went to Rome, where your subject matter changed because it was much more urban there?*

A: While we were in Florence we made a few trips to Venice and I got interested in Giorgione and in Bellini and Carpaccio; I know they affected me. Anyway, in Rome we lived in the American Academy. That was a particular kind of social situation, and that's when the work started going in the direction of the pornographic pictures.

Q: *Why do you call them pornographic?*

A: It's just a label. They're really not pornographic. They're antipornographic. They may be pornographic if you drew up a technical definition — probably having to do with genitalia. But it comes out motivated more by a kind of horror of sex rather than a sensual approach to it. Now, as I look back, I see that kind of painting as a kind of social act. Working at the Academy was a kind of catalyst for a lot of repressed anger which sooner or later I guess I had to try to work through.

Q: *Were you provoked by the gentility of the Academy? Were you reacting against it, or were you reacting to the life going on around you?*

A: Against a part of it. Anyway, you're not interested in showing the more bizarre aspect of that stuff.

Q: *Well, let's just say I prefer not to make an issue of something which might divert attention from the total character of your work. I think our selection represents you well, in all phases.*

A: Looking back I think that some of those paintings are interesting, but it seems so to me now only to the extent that it was an extreme movement in that direction — as far as I went with it. But people see that same sexual impulse in a lot of the current things — like in some of the still lifes and in a lot of the forms I invent. To me it's very interesting to see how that impulse which is so blatant, almost as a kind of illustration in the early work, then reappears years later in a much more complex and subtle way.

Q: *You were a painter of landscapes celebrating nature in Florence, and suddenly you were into another kind of subject in Rome.*

A: I remember thinking that the real theme of the people in the landscapes was alienation. That the people never quite fit into the landscapes. That's the way I felt then. It's a recurrent theme that runs through all the paintings. But it was more conscious and deliberate in the landscapes when I was doing it then. Your know, I was a young painter, working more at the top layers. People hanging around landscape. They're not integrated into a landscape the way a Renaissance mind would do it. It was playing with that theme — "I don't fit here," or "I'm alienated."

Q: *Well, to jump from Italy back to America, do you feel that your subject has changed again as a result of your being in a new environment, or perhaps I should say, back in an old environment?*

A: When I came back to America in 1970 we lived in the country in Massachusetts and I started doing landscapes, and there were a lot of paintings I did of Northampton — local things. I became very attached again to the old genre impulse. I was fascinated by the local character and flavor of that part of America. It was very new and fresh to me. I loved the photographs of the local scenes in the Northampton newspapers. I felt I was seeing the truly strange and bizarre in the ordinary and everyday news photo.

Q: *Was it at all influenced by what was going on in painting here? You know, late Pop and Photorealism?*

A: No, not really. It was about this time that my wife started really developing her own painting, and it was very exciting because we pushed each other a lot in the direction of realism and in looking at nature. She was primarily responsible for my moving away from the small-scale photopaintings toward the life-size portraits and still lifes that I started doing then. We have always had a dynamic and active effect on each other's work — and we have been relentless in keeping each other's standards as high as we dared.

Q: *I am very curious to know to what degree the ambience you live in — whether it's the landscape, the people, the architecture — what effect do you think it has on your work?*

A: Well, the Italian stuff obviously is just soaked with the textures of Italy — the feeling, the colors. But now I'm doing a lot of things in the studio. The last three paintings have been self-portraits and still lifes.

Q: *Does the environment here impose fewer pressures — are you less aware of its presence and therefore able to retreat into a more personal involvement than when you were in Rome?*

A: I don't know. Maybe it's a question of age; I'm forty now. Probably most painters start off being more romantic, and later things just get more balanced. I wanted to do moody landscapes. When I was younger I just spent more time on the outside looking around, and if I had been living in New York twelve years ago I'm sure I would have been open to what was in the streets. Maybe if I were living in Italy now I'd be spending most of my time in the studio looking at myself in the mirror, or at a few strange-looking vegetables, as I've done here for the last few years.

Q: *Where did you study in New York?*

A: Cooper Union, from 1954 to 1960. And later in San Francisco.

Q: *What made you go to San Francisco? Was there any special reason?*

A: It was the school. Cooper Union was a three-year school at that time, but it didn't give a degree, and I wanted the degree. A lot of Cooper people went up to Yale for that extra year. But a bunch of us went out to San Francisco instead.

Q: *I gather that you didn't look forward to Yale because of certain attitudes at the art school there. Instead, you went to San Francisco to study at the Art Institute. As I remember from the Gruen article [Art News 76 (March 1977): 78-81], you studied with Diebenkorn.*

A: Yes, briefly. Also Bischoff, Lobdell, and others. But I wasn't really close to any of them. They probably don't remember me. But it was a good place to paint. A lot of devoted students, a very exciting atmosphere. Bischoff ran the Masters' program and it was very intense for a lot of us.

Q: *Well, was there anybody out there who motivated you, or directed you, or inspired you in any way? Teachers are supposed to do that.*

A: I know, but it didn't happen to me. Not really. I was painting tight, and they all believed in spontaneity, openness, and surprise — coming out of the big brush. Nevertheless, they respected what I was doing and encouraged me to be my own painter.

Q: *In Italy, you say you were affected by the old masters. Do you feel they affected your work to such a degree that you could say truly that a particular artist influenced you? Many people have felt on looking at your pictures that they have a Northern rather than a Mediterranean quality.*

A: It was the Northern Italian painters I liked, and of course, Dürer, Grünewald. But it was the Northern Italians, like Mantegna, who affected me most. My favorite Italian painter still is Carlo Crivelli. I think he's absolutely — he's the one more than anybody else, Carlo Crivelli. And then there were other strange ones, like Ercole Roberti — you know, kind of a very odd painter. Not the later Venetians like Tintoretto, but the Germans and the Flemish and, as I said, the Northern Italians.

Q: *That's interesting about Crivelli. There is something in your work which suggests his use of the niche and the ledge in which he set his compositions. And the drawing.*

A: Yes, and the sense of volume. And the tempera technique — a technique that I'm still using.

Q: *Crivelli was a Gothic artist in the middle of the Renaissance. He retained that sharp bite which we associate more with the Gothic than with the Renaissance.*

A: He's one of the few painters that you can look at and ask, "Do you suppose that thing is real?" He has one painting where there is a hatchet in a saint's head, and the hatchet was sculpted in plaster of paris, actually modeled in relief. It's sculptural. But you know, right next to it will be the hand, painted. Or the head. And both techniques work on the same perceptual level. He was that good. The relief became the standard he had to achieve in his rendering.

Q: *That image of the hatchet. I notice that similar types of images of evisceration and laceration come up again and again in your works. People are bruised, or they're injured, or they're lacerated. There's one terrifying picture of a head with blood just gushing out.*

A: That was *War Shrine*, an antiwar piece. It's the only one of my works that was created to have social significance.

Q: *But there are people whose faces are cut up or bruised. And there's the amputated* Woman on Blue Ground *[cat. no. 30]. Were you seeing people who were physically maimed like that?*

A: No. They're metaphors for the pain. Psychic pain. People don't seem to notice it, but Western art is full of it. It's a predominant theme in Christian art. Saints, martyrs, people being crucified, tortured — but people don't see that content because the Christian theme neutralizes it. You say, "Oh, that's Christ, or that's Saint Paul — I know that story." But if you look at Renaissance art, Christian art, what percentage of the paintings do you think involve somebody being assaulted? You know? A whole lot of Christian art.

Q: *So you see yourself as following in that tradition?*

A: Not really. But some of those paintings had a great impact on me. I remember a big painting in two parts by Petrus Christus I saw in Bruges. The first part shows the mayor of a town sitting on a throne and people are accusing him of taking a bribe. The second part of the painting shows his punishment — to be skinned alive. It was a huge painting, and it was meticulously done. It was *beautifully* done. Everybody's face, and every drop of blood. It showed he was still alive and they were ripping the skin off, and he's in terrible anguish, screaming. It has an impact, a painting like that. Really an impact. It wouldn't have an impact if it weren't well painted, you know, if somebody did the painting loose. But the contrast between the loving care of the technique and the subject matter has a very strong impact.

Q: *Your own metaphors certainly have a very direct and an abrupt impact on the viewer. But to paint the way you do I imagine that you've got to work methodically, very deliberately figuring each step, being almost clinical about it. Isn't there some disparity in such violent subjects and then carefully, quietly, rationally working them out in detail?*

A: Well, you make an image that's not really all that accurate. It's not that clear when you begin. I know painters who do work like that. They work with their intellect mostly. No matter what the subject matter is, they start in the upper left-hand corner and work from there. I don't know how Petrus Christus or Memling painted. But I do know painters who are very detached, and I don't paint like that. All the paintings you're talking about went through changes, and there was emotional involvement. What you're saying is also true to a degree; but it's not a cold approach either. And it's not detachment. What I'm saying is that it's not as extreme as you put it, where the subject matter is one thing and the technique and the rendering is another. It's not like that. The fact that I'm painting a wound, even though I'm doing it with a small brush, doesn't mean that I'm being clinical. I think you're confusing ends and means.

Q: *Perhaps, but in a sense you're creating the wound.*

A: Yes, that kind of thing. It's a living thing, painting. It's a living process. It's anthropomorphic. It's a sort of identification, a kind of wound, and if I'm painting the inside of a wound it feels different than if I were painting on the surface of some other thing. It's a very intuitive, emotional process.

Q: *It must be exhausting . . . . When I first looked at your paintings I was struck by their ferocity. They seemed to me to be full of brutality and aggressiveness. And yet, as I became more absorbed in them, I sensed more and more sadness and hurt . . . suffering, a quiet and chronic suffering in the paintings, rather than some cataclysmic event of destruction in which there is a beginning and an end to that event.*

A: I think that's true. The feeling of being trapped. My background was Catholic and I grew up in a very restricted and repressed social environment in New Jersey. And there's a lot of anguish and pain in that. Like a delicate organism being born in the world and the kind of *violence* that's done to it as a matter of course.

Q: *The first thing you do is slap a baby the minute it comes into the world.*

A: Yes. That kind of violence, that attitude which I symbolize in my approach is reinforced by parents, by the school, and by the Church. And they're all coming down on a mind, a consciousness, you know? It's a very painful thing.

Q: *Are you Catholic now? Do you go to church?*

A: No.

Q: *Have you renounced it? I mean, consciously?*

A: Yes, violently. Like Catholics tend to do. It took me a long time because I was brought up in a place where I was surrounded by a sea of Catholics.

Q: *A papal see . . . .*

A: [Laughter] I mean, some people drift away from religion. But for me it was like an obsessive challenge, a debate. I was always arguing religion when I was in high school. And it was very hard—I had to fight my way through it. It took me a long time.

Q: *Are your paintings religious?*

A: Yes, the paintings are religious—like the erotic paintings are religious. Definitely. Because they come out of repression. They come out of a dramatic reaction to repression. They come out of the impulse to do sacrilege, which is a religious impulse. It's ironic that I did those paintings not far from St. Peter's. And I did get into some trouble with them. They were shown in Italy because I *wanted* to show them there particularly. So I put them in a show, and somebody gouged one of them. It wasn't even a very erotic one—just a painting of two standing nudes, two sisters. One had on a bathrobe, the other was nude [*Two Women* (cat. no. 13)]. Anyway, exhibiting it was playing out that *melodrama* of regressing and getting the reaction. You get the urge to sacrilege when you begin to get relatively free of it. But that's the negative side of it, of the religious thing. But the paintings I'm doing now still seem to me very religious in another sense. I don't have to do the shocking paintings any more because I'm through

24

with them. But now—and this is what a lot of people don't see, and it really annoys me—now the paintings are moving toward religiousness in a positive sense.

Q: *When you say that you've renounced the Church and settled in your own mind what your feelings are, does that coincide with or parallel the the development of your painting?*

A: Well, not chronologically. There's overlap.

Q: *No. I didn't mean all at once, or that you began painting a certain way. But is there an analogous situation?*

A: Not specifically to the Church. Getting rid of the ideas of original sin and heaven and hell, that was the intellectual battle I got over when I was about eighteen. It didn't make sense to me any more intellectually because I moved into another cultural environment—art school, and books, and philosophy. And I could say all that other stuff didn't make sense at all. I rejected all the religious doctrines and became free of them. Intellectually. But emotionally there's still a twenty-year impact on your feelings and on the way your mind works unconsciously—repression, and fears, and *guilt.* Maybe you never get over it completely. Intellectually I'm one thing, emotionally I'm something else. It creates a kind of schizophrenia which art—painting—is able to express. My art is based on contradiction; there's nothing simple in it. It's always multiple.

Q: *If your earlier paintings are preoccupied with certain negative aspects of life—in creating these scenes, these little scenarios, or these little melodramas as you call them, how do you arrive at them? Are they from literary sources? Do you, for instance, read a scene that you then decide to paint? For instance, something like the painting called* Three Sisters *[cat. no. 31].*

A: They were all done starting with photographs. I'd take a photograph from a newspaper or a magazine. And I would paint figures out—I would change the scene. I would "Rorschach" into the scene, you know? Certain figures would be painted out, other figures would be left in. Then I would collage other figures in, so it would be composed. Then I would undress some of them. Or I would add things. Some of them are sexually very explicit. It was a kind of improvisation that came out of adolescent and repressed sexuality.

    I used to have a box full of little figures from photographs that I cut out and used to compose the paintings. Many of the figures in the pictures of piazzas and street scenes were collaged in like that. I'd mix them a hundred times until the arrangement looked interesting. Then I would paste them in. Later on I didn't do that—I'd either trace them or copy them.

Q: *Then this is why many of the earlier works are so small.*

A: Exactly. The size was determined by the photographs. They actually become the image—its underlayer. In fact, while I was living in Florence I showed some paintings at the National

Institute in New York, and they gave me an award, and Emily Genauer wrote a review [*New York Herald Tribune,* May 24, 1964, p. 33] in which she said she wondered whether the people who gave me this award knew what I was really doing. Because when nobody was in the room she went up and touched the paintings, and she was surprised that there were photographs pasted in them. She said she didn't know if anybody knew that, because if they did they probably wouldn't have given me the award! [Laughter]

Q: *I understood you to say that after a while you didn't use the photographs. Instead, you outlined them or traced them. Then how did you succeed in getting the kind of accuracy which the photograph itself suggested? Simply by painting?*

A: Yes. At first, when I began painting, it would have been hard for me to paint a photograph. But later I just got technically good enough so that it was pretty easy.

Q: *But when you painted directly on photographs, in most cases you transformed them?*

A: Yes.

Q: *Let's talk about self-portraits. Do you have any particular feeling about self-portraits as a record of your feelings, your progress through life? Or are they a simple excursion into a format which is easily available?*

A: The expediency of the situation is what starts it, but then it becomes more. It becomes meditation, looking at that image in the mirror. It becomes more fascinating precisely because the mind is looking at the outside, at the flesh, and observing its own exterior. And wondering how to translate that experience in the most intelligent way. Sometimes I think that I could paint the self-portrait from now on, exclusively.

Q: *Rembrandt and others were preoccupied with the self-portrait throughout their lives. With Rembrandt one has the feeling that his self-portraits were a succession of psychological observations from beginning to end. Do you get the feeling that your portraits can be arranged in such a sequence? They're all intense, but some are more intense than others. And some seem more concentrated on your ability to capture the physical reality. Are you aware of this, or is it simply a happenstance?*

A: I'm sure Rembrandt didn't calculate the development you describe; it just came out of the brush. The early self-portraits that I did seemed real to me at that time. Now they look flat and distorted. They don't look anything like me. But at the time that was as real as I could make it.

Q: *Then you're saying that you weren't trying to mirror a specific psychological condition, but rather that you were trying to make a faithful representation of yourself, that you were really registering your vision. And whatever came out of it was not a deliberate attempt to mirror your state of mind.*

A: That's right, although in the early paintings I could see it would be happening, that it might be getting too morbid. But I would play it out, let it go. I was less faithful. The more I painted, though, the more I disciplined myself not to deviate from what I saw, really trusting in direct observation and not letting subjectivity falsify it. In the *Self-Portrait in Studio* [cat. no. 73] I'm doing now, I'm using a magnifying mirror. I was at a point where I couldn't develop this painting; I had been looking in the mirror, and it was getting harder and harder. But then I happened upon an ordinary magnifying mirror in the hardware store and it was just what I needed. The painting has just developed fantastically since then. Sometimes it'll be something like that, a mirror that magnifies better, or a better light. For example, I got a kind of fluorescent light that I can pull right down over the image I'm working on. It has a swivel on it. So the magnifying mirror, plus the better light, enables me to get in and almost see the pores.
In the painting I have a sweater on, and I was able to paint each knit almost. To me, painting the knit—there's as much reality in that as in painting the face.

Q: *You draw no distinction between different kinds of reality, different kinds of objects? You paint the face with the same intensity—or at least with the same care—as you would what you are wearing, or the wall behind you?*

A: Yes. That is my understanding of it. The reality beyond our senses. There is a unity to it on levels that we ordinarily do not experience subjectively.

Q: *It is difficult to ask this of the artist—but how do you account for the fact that you set out to paint what you have in front of you and produce something which is certainly not photographic, and has an intensity which is unique? Do you have any control over that? I don't imagine that you set out by saying to yourself, "I'm going to make this object very intense. Or very strange." You have said here that you only want to paint what you see.*

A: Well, that's true. That's what I try to do. But I know that you can't really paint pores. It is too complex. Even with a magnifying mirror there's a point where you can't see any more. And the brushes are clumsy. I work with a triple zero brush, which is the smallest brush I've been able to find. But if you paint with that brush under a magnifying glass, you see it's really clumsy. Sometimes I *wish* I could have a brush that is better than that, smaller than that. But maybe it is really my mind which resists going further right now. Anyway—in the early paintings when I would begin to lose the accuracy and the painting would develop a strangeness, I'd say, "That's interesting—I think I'll follow that, I'll pursue that. I think I'll let that happen." It wouldn't be calculated beforehand, but as it would happen I would approve of it. And then say, "Well, the hell with reality."

Q: *Why then is accuracy so important to you? Do you feel that in painting things very accurately that you're arriving at a very special truth?*

A: Yes, I do. I really do. And I think it's often been true in art. It's the naturalistic impulse, going back to observing carefully. It always revitalizes art. Much of the weak art in the past resulted from the loss of reality, when the artist stopped observing nature—how things were actually happening. You can always tell when a figurative artist is working from his observations. Life always has these amazing surprises. The imagination tends to feed on itself and its store of memories. Of course, the great thing is to have both sources working together — complementing each other.

Q: *But there are degrees of looking. For example, you cannot deny that Turner looked very, very carefully, or Monet for that matter. And yet, what they produced was anything but careful painting. In fact, it motivated others to look beyond careful painting into other aspects of art.*

A: Well, when I saw the Monets — the ones that had an impact on me, the lilies — it was like getting the impact of a fresh look at nature. I'm not saying it is always tight rendering, but that it is really looking, without having art in the way, the art of the past, the conventions.

Q: *Would there be a difference between looking at your sweater under a microscope and looking at a very careful and precise painting of your sweater?*

A: Well, if you saw my sweater under a microscope, you'd see a reality that we can't pick up with our eyes. I can't paint that. But I can *suggest* it. My painting isn't actually an accurate rendering of *just* what I see. There is a play. This is why I don't like words, because I find myself lying. I want to defend a point, and I realize while I'm doing it that it's not really true, that there's another side to it. It's more complicated than the simple, logical thing. You *can't* paint nature; there's no way of doing it. There's no way of making a replica, of reproducing something which is infinite, which just goes on forever.

Q: *And which changes constantly.*

A: I don't know who said it, but when you really start looking very hard, and trying to get it down, you can go mad, because it's impossible. Paint in no way can compare with living tissue. Paint is inert. It stays put, more or less. It is madness, as I have been told many times, to even think in these terms. But there's this idea in the back of my mind that the harder you try, the better the painting is. Even if it's impossible. Anyway, it doesn't make you crazy, because everyone understands it is only an illusion, a game. It is make-believe.

Q: *The tendency in the last fifty years at least has been to get away from the exact portrayal of nature. You are obviously in disagreement. Are you at all intrigued by Cubism? Do you find yourself interested in Expressionist painting? There have been figurative artists in our time who, instead of trying to capture reality by duplicating appearance, have deliberately sought to transform what they see into a state of emotion, a state of feeling. Do you find value in that kind of work at all? Or is it simply that you don't feel it is for you?*

A: Well, I once found it interesting. For example, I like Morandi. I can look at his work and enjoy the poetry of it, and it's hardly exact rendering. . . .

Q: *Well, how do you feel about Kirchner, or Kokoschka?*

A: I used to like them, years ago — I could like them again.

Q: *But not now?*

A: What you were saying about my trying to render reality but that my emotion or some feeling gets into it almost without my wanting it to—that's kind of what I like. I think the reason is that I don't really believe that surfaces are reality. My mind doubts that very much. I know that there are other structures of reality existing there at the same time that we can't see. I know that, and I want that to be in the painting too. So it's not simple at all. There are always contradictory notions. There's always conflict in the painting. There's a wanting to make it as real as possible, but not *believing* in it at the same time. I know that my flesh is made of chemicals and molecules. I know that what I'm seeing is like a dream. I know that consciousness is something else, but somehow connected to this physical/chemical plane. There is a crazy sort of bewilderment that we all seem to live in—not knowing really what is happening or how it could possibly be happening.

Q: *But you're nevertheless trying to fix the image that you do see—whatever you can control with your human vision?*

A: Yes, but I want to *suggest* that it's not real. In the piece I'm working on now, *Self-Portrait in Studio* [cat. no. 73], I'm painting the pores, but they're beginning to arrange in such a pattern that they suggest movement—just a suggestion of underlying movement.

Q: *Is it because, underlying all that extreme accuracy, there's always an ambiguity or perhaps even an improbability in measuring reality?*

A: Yes. I want it to imply all that.

Q: *I'm interested in your self-portraits because not too many artists are painting themselves these days, or trying to examine themselves with the kind of intensity your pictures show. It's as if you were asking, "What am I? What do I look like? Who am I?" Is it your intention to comprehend the total human enigma by looking so closely at yourself?*

A: Well, something like that. I was thinking just yesterday that I feel maybe my function is really to observe myself. If I can do that very, very well, and very accurately, and very honestly, then I will have done something that's not just myself. It's not really my flesh, and it's not even really my consciousness. You know what I mean? If I can discipline myself to that degree, then in a way it's useful for anyone who's moving along a similar path. The point about change and permanence—in *Still Life with Squash and Rutabagas* [cat. no. 69] I try to imply impermanence, or changing reality. When you go up close to the rutabagas or some of the other still lifes, there's a molecular feeling to the things—a feeling of movement. In *Self-Portrait (Torso)* [cat. no. 66], when you look at the torso for a long time you can feel the blood vessels, you can almost see a thousand little blood vessels underneath the flesh. You have to really stare at it a long time. But it's all there. It's not just this one solid thing; it's a suggestion of veils, that things are happening underneath. And the face is not one expression either. However, for me the painting is not a success unless these all add up to a sense of colossal mass.

Something really solid and substantial. I like it when from ten feet it looks solid and three-dimensional—from five feet you begin to doubt it, and up close you get lost in the beauty of another illusion completely that refers to the microscopic and, perhaps, somehow the spiritual.

Q: *These are issues that don't concern the contemporary painters, most of whom have forfeited the notion of observing reality. Isn't it the figurative painter who is faced with this problem of permanence and impermanence, life and death and so on to a greater degree?*

A: Well, not even too many of *them.* Because most artists who paint figurative paintings approach them from more formal aspects. They are not interested in this kind of thing. They probably find it irrelevant, too metaphysical.

Q: *You are very concerned with thematic content—with your intent to transform, to enlarge upon, the usual and apparent meaning of your subjects. It's true even with some of the still lifes or the genre pictures, like* Northampton Motor Vehicle Department [*cat. no. 40*]. *By the time you're finished with it, it turns out to look like a scene out of Hades.*

A: Well, I think it's always that same theme of ambiguity, of situations not making sense. It's almost like being in a dream. I'm sure a lot of people have experienced that—it's not unique to me. But it's often struck me that some of these paintings came out of experiences I had when I was young. My mother was mentally ill, she had been in asylums all during my childhood—ever since I was in second grade. We used to visit her every week and it was a world which made a great impression on me—people wandering around. The same feeling often recurs when I'm in public places or in social settings. It's like a huge insane asylum where people have costumes on and they're doing their routine and I'm doing mine. And I sometimes get this incredible feeling of insecurity. Often I like to get that feeling in the painting without making it too obvious. Some of those [early] paintings are too obvious and I don't like them any more. I guess I would call them failures.

Q: *They're only failures to you at this moment; I think they're extraordinary.*

A: Anyway, I like it much better when it's really under the surface. Like when I paint rutabagas or self-portraits, and it's really packed underneath with tension. Underneath.

Q: *You've said in the Gruen interview that in your early days as a painter your work did not "fit in" with the gestural, painterly intentions of the prevailing New York School, nor with the thickly painted pictures of the California School. Now that figurative painting has once again become an accepted style, do you feel more a sense of belonging? Do you feel that your dedication has been justified and that you're more comfortable in the art world, instead of being isolated and an outsider?*

A: I suppose I never really moved around a lot in the art world, but that doesn't bother me too much. I just kind of centered all my energy on painting, and I was supported and encouraged to do that by Bella Fishko, whose gallery has shown my work from the beginning. She always encouraged me to concentrate on my work and not get too distracted by the art world, and I guess that's what I've always done.

Gillespie's working method has frequently entailed profound changes in the content of given paintings, even years after they have been dated and presumed complete, and some works have been exhibited in various states of completion, occasionally with differing titles in the various states. In a few cases a small painting may have been physically incorporated into a larger one, and subsequently may have been replaced by yet another. In other cases, even the dimensions of paintings have changed as the artist has sawed down or added onto their wood supports.

For this catalogue all titles have been approved by the artist and sometimes represent a clarification of previous titles for the same works; where new titles have been assigned, the previously published titles have been noted. Dimensions, as supplied by lenders, are in inches, height by width by depth. Except where provenance is noted, works were acquired by lenders directly from the artist or his dealers in the United States or Italy. Selected references are included where appropriate. The artist's commentaries are extracts from an interview with him by Abram Lerner and Howard Fox at the Hirshhorn Museum and Sculpture Garden on March 24, 1977.

H.F.

1. **Allegorical Street Scene**
   1961-62, repainted in 1963
   Oil on paper mounted on wood
   9 x 7⅜

   Collection:
   Hirshhorn Museum and
   Sculpture Garden

   Provenance:
   Joseph H. Hirshhorn, 1966

   Exhibited:
   The National Institute of Arts
   and Letters, New York. "An
   Exhibition of Contemporary
   Painting, Sculpture and Graphic
   Art." March 13-29, 1964.

   The American Academy of Arts
   and Letters and The National
   Institute of Arts and Letters, New
   York. "Exhibition of Work by
   Newly Elected Members and
   Recipients of Honors and
   Awards." May 20-August 30, 1964.

   Forum Gallery, New York.
   "Gregory Gillespie: First One
   Man Exhibition." February 15-26,
   1966.

"An allegory is a parable, or a fable, where the figures represent something else. I was playing with the idea that things were ambiguous, that they didn't make sense. Italian art, religious art looked that way to me. I didn't know who St. Francis was giving a gold cup to, or what each specific scene meant. I'd just be looking at paintings, yet I didn't know the Christian myths. I felt painting didn't really have to make sense on that level. I don't think I believe that anymore.

"I'm not sure now what this picture means. I was intrigued by the male-female theme. The herm-aphroditic theme is connected with my idea of the artist, perhaps with all of us. It's a theme I played with a lot. I thought at that time that the artist had to unite both.

"That figure in the doorway reoccurs in the paintings. There's a figure lurking in the background in several paintings, peering in at the scene. Probably it represents a part of me—the voyeur, the spectator, the observer, the disembodied one. He's the artist —the one who observes."

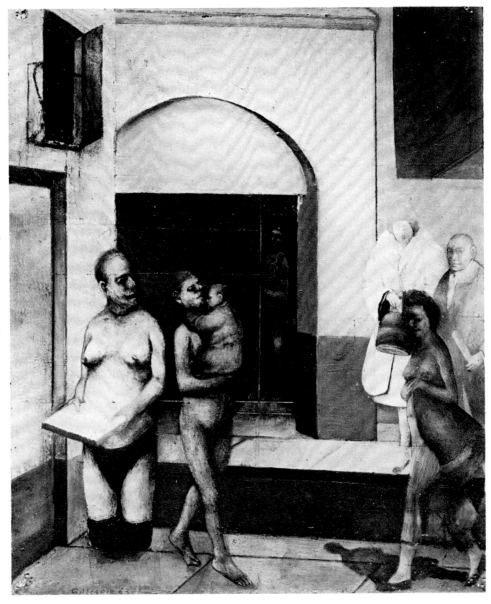

2. Two Men Seated
1961-62
Oil on wood
9⅜ x 10⅞

Collection:
Hirshhorn Museum and
Sculpture Garden

Provenance:
Joseph H. Hirshhorn, 1966

Exhibited:
The National Institute of Arts
and Letters, New York. "An
Exhibition of Contemporary
Painting, Sculpture and Graphic
Art." March 13-29, 1964.

The American Academy of Arts
and Letters and The National
Institute of Arts and Letters,
New York. "Exhibition of Work
by Newly Elected Members and
Recipients of Honors and
Awards." May 20-August 30,
1964.

Forum Gallery, New York.
"Gregory Gillespie: First One
Man Exhibition." February
15-26, 1966.

Hirshhorn Museum and
Sculpture Garden, Washington,
D.C. "Inaugural Exhibition."
October 4, 1974-October 16,
1975. [Not listed in catalogue.]

3. Bathers in a Landscape

[also called *Two People Bathing in a Landscape* and *Woman Bathing in a Landscape*]
1962
Oil on wood
8¼ x 9⅜

Collection:
Hirshhorn Museum and Sculpture Garden

Provenance:
Joseph H. Hirshhorn, 1966

Exhibited:
The National Institute of Arts and Letters, New York. "An Exhibition of Contemporary Painting, Sculpture and Graphic Art." March 13-29, 1964.

The American Academy of Arts and Letters and The National Institute of Arts and Letters, New York. "Exhibition of Work by Newly Elected Members and Recipients of Honors and Awards." May 20-August 30, 1964.

Forum Gallery, New York. "Gregory Gillespie: First One Man Exhibition." February 15-26, 1966.

Hirshhorn Museum and Sculpture Garden, Washington, D.C. "Inaugural Exhibition." October 4, 1974–October 16, 1975. [Not listed in catalogue.]

"This painting has one of those figures that recurs all the time in my work—a woman walking away. She's even in the paintings I was working on just recently. For whatever it's worth, I always assumed it was an image of my mother."

4. Landscape at Night
[also called *Night Landscape*]
1962–63
Mixed media
10 x 12

Collection:
Daniel Selznick, Los Angeles

Exhibited:
The National Institute of Arts and Letters, New York. "An Exhibition of Contemporary Painting, Sculpture and Graphic Art." March 13-29, 1964.

The American Academy of Arts and Letters and The National Institute of Arts and Letters, New York. "Exhibition of Work by Newly Elected Members and Recipients of Honors and Awards." May 20-August 30, 1964.

Forum Gallery, New York "Gregory Gillespie: First One Man Exhibition." February 15-26, 1966.

Forum Gallery, New York. "Gregory Gillespie: First One Man Exhibition." February 15-26, 1966.

The Alpha Gallery, Boston. "Gregory Gillespie: Paintings." April 10-May 1, 1971.

5. Imaginary Self-Portrait
[also called *Portrait of a Man*]
1963
Oil on wood
20 x 18

Collection:
Private collection

Exhibited:
The American Academy of Arts and Letters and The National Institute of Arts and Letters, New York. "Exhibition of Work by Newly Elected Members and Recipients of Honors and Awards." May 20–August 30, 1964.

Forum Gallery, New York. "Gregory Gillespie: First One Man Exhibition." February 15–26, 1966.

6. Piazza at Night
1963–64
Oil and magazine photographs
on wood
11 x 9⅞

Collection:
William A. Gumberts, Evansville,
Indiana

Exhibited:
The American Academy of Arts
and Letters and The National
Institute of Arts and Letters,
New York. "Exhibition of Work
by Newly Elected Members and
Recipients of Honors and
Awards." May 20–August 30,
1964.

Forum Gallery, New York.
"Gregory Gillespie: First One
Man Exhibition." February
15–26, 1966.

7. Street in Madrid
1963
Oil and magazine photographs
on wood
10¾ x 10

Collection:
Bella and Sol Fishko, New York

Exhibited:
Forum Gallery, New York.
"Gregory Gillespie: First One
Man Exhibition." February
15-26, 1966.

Flint Institute of Arts, Flint,
Michigan. "Realism Revisited:
Fifty Years of American Realistic
Painting Since the Armory
Show." April 28-May 29, 1966.

Georgia Museum of Art, The
University of Georgia, Athens.
"Gregory Gillespie."
October-November 1970.

The Alpha Gallery, Boston.
"Gregory Gillespie: Paintings."
April 10-May 1, 1971.

*"The technique is photocollage. You can see the outlines in some of the
figures. You know the Balthus street scenes? It came out of those."*

8. Roman Landscape (Picnic)
[also called *Landscape with Three Nude Bathers*]
c. 1963
Oil and magazine photographs
on wood
5¾ x 8½

Collection:
Mr. and Mrs. James M. Sampson,
Hingham, Massachusetts

Exhibited:
The National Institute of Arts
and Letters, New York. "An
Exhibition of Contemporary
Painting, Sculpture and Graphic
Art." March 13-29, 1964.

The American Academy of Arts
and Letters and The National

Institute of Arts and Letters, New
York. "Exhibition of Work by
Newly Elected Members and
Recipients of Honors and
Awards." May 20-August 30,
1964.

American Academy in Rome.
"Gregory Gillespie: Quadri
Recenti." December 15,
1969-January 7, 1970.

Forum Gallery, New York.
"Gregory Gillespie." February
14-March 10, 1970.

Georgia Museum of Art, The
University of Georgia, Athens.
"Gregory Gillespie."
October-November 1970.

*"This is a strange picnic, and it looks like they're moonbathing. But
they are sunbathing nonetheless. . . . I don't choose my titles in order to
create an ambiguous meaning."*

9. Street in Spain
1964
Oil and magazine photographs
on wood
7¼ x 10¾

Collection:
Daniel Selznick, Los Angeles

Exhibited:
Forum Gallery, New York.
"Gregory Gillespie: First One
Man Exhibition." February
15-26, 1966.

The Alpha Gallery, Boston.
"Gregory Gillespie: Paintings."
April 10-May 1, 1971.

10. Street in Rome
1965
Oil and magazine photographs
on wood
9½ x 7

Collection:
Mr. and Mrs. John Wasserman,
New York

Exhibited:
Forum Gallery, New York.
"Gregory Gillespie: First One
Man Exhibition." February
15-26, 1966.

11. Woman Walking in a Room
1965
Oil and magazine photographs
on wood
10¾ x 14

Collection:
Bella and Sol Fishko, New York

Provenance:
William Dorr, 1971

Exhibited:
American Academy in Rome.
"Annual Exhibition of Painting,
Sculpture and Architecture."
Spring 1965.

Whitney Museum of American
Art, New York. "1965 Annual
Exhibition of Contemporary
American Painting." December
8, 1965-January 30, 1966.

Forum Gallery, New York.
"Gregory Gillespie: First One
Man Exhibition." February
15-26, 1966.

The Alpha Gallery, Boston.
"Gregory Gillespie: Paintings."
April 10-May 1, 1971.

Smith College Museum of Art,
Smith College, Northampton,
Massachusetts. "Gregory
Gillespie: Recent Paintings."
November 18-December 23,
1971.

Duke University Museum of
Art, Durham, North Carolina.

[Exhibited during Gillespie's
participation in Visiting Artists
Program sponsored by the
Department of Art and the
Undergraduate Teaching
Council.] Week of January 26,
1976.

Reference:
Gendel, Milton. "Art News from
Italy." *Art News* 64 (September
1965): 59.

"She was a model I photographed. I don't think I collaged her in — I copied the photograph
and placed her in a setting, which was a picture of an Italian barber shop that I took from a magazine.
There were barber chairs and other stuff which I painted out. I just kept the room, painted in
a new floor, and placed her in it. There's actually very little left of the photographic
image except the stuff in the corner.

"I think there's some sort of magnetic pull between the objects and herself, an anticipation; it's a
subtle psychological thing. It may have to do with the briefcase and the round box being closed —
the sense that there is an object of significance in that corner."

12. Woman In Brassiere
1965
Mixed media
6½ x 6¼

Collection:
Bella and Sol Fishko, New York

Provenance:
Harold Merklen, 1972

Exhibited:
Forum Gallery, New York.
"Gregory Gillespie: First One
Man Exhibition." February
15-26, 1966.

"There's that same woman in profile [see cat. no. 11]. She's very related to me, like that lady with the jewels [see cat. no. 23]. The brassiere is like a clamp. I'm pretty sure that when I've painted clothing like that it signified the idea of repression — the notion of the flesh being constricted."

13. Two Women
1965
Mixed media
14 x 11

Collection:
Whitney Museum of American Art, New York; Gift of the Friends of the Whitney Museum of American Art

Exhibited:
Galleria Feltrinelli, Rome. "13 pittore ospiti di Roma" ("13 Painters Sojourning in Rome"). July 1965.[?]

Forum Gallery, New York. "Gregory Gillespie: First One Man Exhibition." February 15–26, 1966.

Whitney Museum of American Art, New York. "Recent Acquisitions." May 23–July 7, 1968.

Whitney Museum of American Art, New York. "Friends' Acquisitions." May 1–24, 1970.

The American Academy of Arts and Letters and The National Institute of Arts and Letters, New York. "Exhibition of Works by Candidates for Art Awards." March 8–April 4, 1976.

The American Academy of Arts and Letters and The National Institute of Arts and Letters, New York. "Exhibition of Work by Newly Elected Members and Recipients of Honors and Awards." May 20–June 13, 1976.

Reference:
Schwartz, Barry. *The New Humanism* (New York: Praeger Publishers), pp. 68–69, colorplate IV.

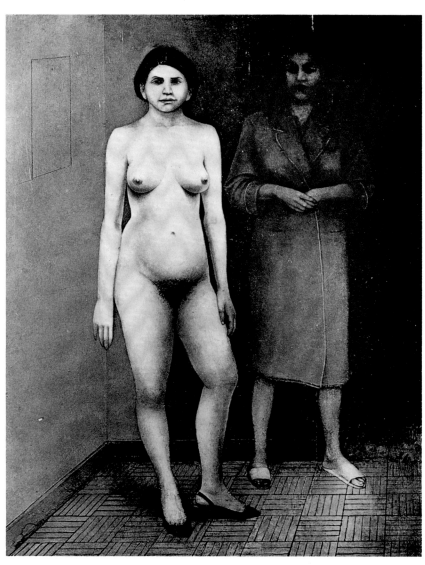

"This is the painting they punctured when it was exhibited in Italy, probably because it showed pubic hair. Italians never paint that. Maybe they do today, but they didn't in the older tradition.

"In the original photograph they were both dressed. No doubt I've changed their relationship by taking her clothes off."

14. Seated Man and Girl
1965–67
Oil and magazine photographs
on wood
8½ x 10¾

Collection:
Rheta Sosland, Shawnee Mission,
Kansas

Exhibited:
Forum Gallery, New York.
"Gregory Gillespie." January
9-26, 1968.

"The man sitting was originally a photograph of Giorgio di Chirico at his easel sitting with a paint brush in his hand, and with his shirt on. The girl was from another source completely."

15. Three People in a Courtyard
1966
Mixed media
7¼ x 7½

Collection:
Mr. and Mrs. John Koch, New York

Exhibited:
Forum Gallery, New York. "Gregory Gillespie: First One Man Exhibition." February 15-26, 1966.

"That's really the way it looked. But I think I meant that little doorway to be something else, like an alcove you put things into. It doesn't necessarily have to be a doorway. You know, in Italy everything was strange, not everything made sense."

16. Trattoria

1966
Mixed media
9½ x 6

Collection:
Bella and Sol Fishko, New York

Exhibited:
Forum Gallery, New York. "Gregory Gillespie." January 9-26, 1968.

Georgia Museum of Art, The University of Georgia, Athens. "Gregory Gillespie." October-November 1970.

The Alpha Gallery, Boston. "Gregory Gillespie: Paintings." April 10-May 1, 1971.

University Gallery, University of Massachusetts, Amherst. "Frances Cohen Gillespie and Gregory Gillespie." September 18-October 13, 1976.

"Those outlines inscribed right into the paint suggest things that might be there, like a table leg; but it didn't have to be represented. I did stuff like that in other works too. Maybe it stayed in the painting for a long time; then I'd take it out with a razor blade, but there would still be traces which I'd leave in. So it's as if it were there, or is there in another dimension. I like that, because it gives a suggestion of time."

17. Roman Interior (Still Life)
[also called *Roman Interior No. 1,* in earlier state of completion]
1966–67
Oil and magazine photographs on wood
43¾ x 33

Collection:
Mr. and Mrs. Jacob M. Kaplan, New York

Exhibited:
Galleria Il Capitello, Rome. "1° Premio Internazionale di Pittura Figurativa 'Richiamo di Roma'" ("First International Competition of Figurative Painting 'Recollections of Rome'"). February 18–March 4, 1967. [Wins Medaglia d'Oro del Senato della Repubblica for *Roman Interior No. 1.*]

Whitney Museum of American Art. "1967 Annual Exhibition of Contemporary American Painting." December 13, 1967–February 4, 1968.

Forum Gallery, New York. "Gregory Gillespie." January 9–26, 1968.

References:
"Painting Prize." *Daily American* (Rome), February 23, 1967, p. 2.

"'Rome Recollections' Win for U. S. Painter." *Daily American* (Rome), February 24, 1967, p. 6.

Lucas, John. "Roman Column: Pedestrians & Poets." *Arts Magazine* 41 (May 1967): 15.

"In Rome I loved the trattorias. I used to hang out in these places. I'd drink, usually by myself, and after the right amount of alcohol it would start to look very powerful. And it did have this melancholy quality, it wasn't a cheerful thing.

"The Castello St. Angelo through the window is probably pasted in from a postcard and then painted over. The can is from Bourbon Cafe – that came from an advertisement. It's a trattoria-shrine idea, with a window and the outside. I loved the trattorias at that time."

18. Trattoria della Piazza di Spagna
1967
Mixed media
40 x 41

Collection:
Private collection

Exhibited:
Forum Gallery, New York.
"Gregory Gillespie." January
9-26, 1968.

19. Landscape
1967
Mixed media
15 ½ x 17 ½

Collection:
Mrs. George Boynton, Tuxedo
Park, New York

Exhibited:
Forum Gallery, New York.
"Gregory Gillespie." January
9–26, 1968.

20. Black Box I
1967
Mixed media
22¾ x 12⅜ x 9¾

Collection:
Joseph H. Hirshhorn,
Washington, D.C.

Exhibited:
Forum Gallery, New York.
"Gregory Gillespie." January
9-26, 1968.

"This was the idea for the Italian shrine paintings. On their graves they often place a photograph of the person who's buried and they fix the photo in plastic, to preserve it. That's a photograph pasted in the box, with many layers of glaze on it. It's a three-dimensional conception, and the thing on the bottom is a hubcap. Again, it's the idea of the religious thing — the relic."

Detail of underside of pedestal.

21. Exterior Wall with Landscape
1967
Mixed media
39⅝ x 25⅝ x 4⅞

Collection:
Hirshhorn Museum and
Sculpture Garden

Provenance:
Joseph H. Hirshhorn, 1972

Exhibited:
Forum Gallery, New York.
"Gregory Gillespie." January
9-26, 1968.

Whitney Museum of American
Art, New York. "Human
Concern/Personal Torment: The
Grotesque in American Art."
October 14–November 30, 1969
(and tour to University Art
Museum, University of
California, Berkeley, January 20–
March 1, 1970).

References:
"Art: Beyond Nightmare." *Time*
93 (June 13, 1969): 74–75.
Psychiatry and Social Science Review
4 (July 14, 1970): front cover.
[Reproduction; no text.]

*"I was just playing with religious
symbols and ideas—the femaleness
and the organic quality of that
stucco wall. You get that in
Rome, the vulnerability of people
living in those cement environments.
Often there's that idyllic landscape
out the window. That oozing
form—that's in other paintings
as well. Maybe it's like our innards
—gall bladder, liver, organs,
organic life. It looks like it's
getting buried in the wall.
The walls were alive to me."*

22. Roman Interior — Kitchen
[also called *Still Life with Milk Carton*]
1967–69, repainted 1976
Mixed media
63 x 45½

Collection:
George Gilbert, New York

Exhibited:
Forum Gallery, New York.
"Gregory Gillespie." February 14–
March 10, 1970.

University Gallery, University of
Massachusetts, Amherst.
"Frances Cohen Gillespie and
Gregory Gillespie." September 18–
October 13, 1976.

Forum Gallery, New York.
"Gregory Gillespie: Recent
Paintings." November 13–
December 4, 1976.

Reference:
Betz, Margaret. "New York
Reviews: Gregory Gillespie." *Art
News* 76 (January 1977): 126.

23. Lady with Jewels
[also called *Woman with Beads*]
c. 1968
Mixed media
6 x 4

Collection:
Private collection

Exhibited:
Forum Gallery, New York.
"Gregory Gillespie." February 14–
March 10, 1970.

"I think this was one of the paintings where I would just paste an image down, and then I'd paint off the clothes—denude the figure, and then add things. When you paint, your motivations are not all that clear.

"This is not sensual. Her body is explicit, but everything is stiff. The clothing represses her. Her teeth are emphasized, but I think that's because I probably lacked the skill to paint a smile convincingly. Her smile looks good because it's also like a snarl. It was a complexity I liked."

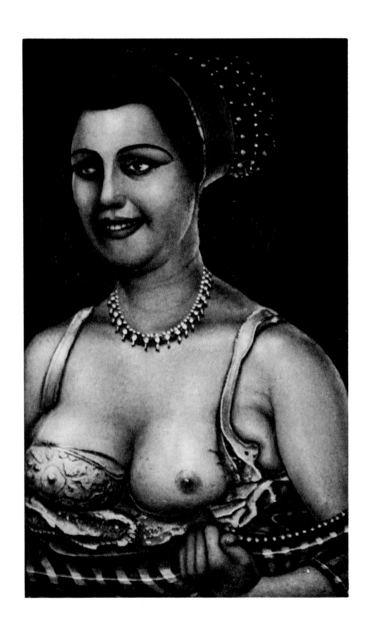

24. Soccer Star
1968
Mixed media
6¼ x 3¾

Collection:
Mr. and Mrs. Peter B. Ornstein,
New York

Exhibited:
Forum Gallery, New York.
"Gregory Gillespie." February 14–
March 10, 1970.

The Alpha Gallery, Boston.
"Gregory Gillespie: Paintings."
April 10–May 1, 1971.

Museum of Art of Ogunquit,
Ogunquit, Maine. "Twentieth
Annual Exhibition." July 1–
September 4, 1972.

"He's a soccer player, and this was a photograph I painted over. I wanted to take a popular snapshot kind of image and then sculpt into it three-dimensionally what ordinarily would not be seen —in this case the interior organs of his body. It's juxtaposing what we know exists but cannot see with what is conventionally seen —in this case a camera image of a popular Italian soccer star."

25. Allegorical Painting (Insects)
1968
Oil and Polaroid film negative
mounted on wood
6½ x 4

Collection:
Mr. and Mrs. Daniel W. Dietrich II,
Chester Springs, Pennsylvania

Exhibited:
Forum Gallery, New York.
"Gregory Gillespie." February 14–
March 10, 1970.

Reference:
Canaday, John. "Art: Dissent at
the Academy of Design." *New
York Times,* February 28, 1970,
p. 25.

*"On the street I once found the paper backing you throw away from
Polaroid film, and it had this brownish kind of stuff in the lines — there
was a pattern in it. It was a very beautiful pattern and suggested these
shapes and creatures. So I took it home and glued it down and I
painted on it."*

26. Woman with Baby (Crying)
1968
Mixed media
7½ x 6½

Collection:
Ira Schwartz, New York

Exhibited:
Galleria La Margherita, Rome.
"Estate 1969" ("Summer 1969").
July 3-August 9, 1969.

Forum Gallery, New York.
"Gregory Gillespie." February 14–
March 10, 1970.

The Alpha Gallery, Boston.
"Gregory Gillespie: Paintings."
April 10-May 1, 1971.

Reference:
Schwartz, Barry. *The New
Humanism* (New York: Praeger
Publishers, 1974), pp. 67-68.

27. Doll-Child
1968
Mixed media
15⅞ x 19¾

Collection:
The University of Georgia,
Georgia Museum of Art, Athens;
Gift of Childe Hassam Fund, The
American Academy of Arts and
Letters, 1971

Exhibited:
Forum Gallery, New York.
"Gregory Gillespie." February 14–
March 10, 1970.

Georgia Museum of Art, The
University of Georgia, Athens.
"Gregory Gillespie."
October–November 1970.

The American Academy of Arts
and Letters, New York.
"Exhibition of Paintings Eligible
for Purchase under the Childe
Hassam Fund." November
12–December 13, 1970. [*Doll-Child*
purchased and presented to the
Georgia Museum of Art.]

28. Self-Portrait in Black Shirt
1968–69
Oil and Magna on wood
11¾ x 9¼

Collection:
Jerome Reich, Boston

Exhibited:
Forum Gallery, New York.
"Gregory Gillespie." February 14–
March 10, 1970.

Georgia Museum of Art, The
University of Georgia, Athens.
"Gregory Gillespie."
October–November 1970.

The Alpha Gallery, Boston.
"Gregory Gillespie: Paintings
April 10–May 1, 1971.

29. Bruised Man (Round Painting)
c. 1969
Oil and magazine photograph on wood
5″ diameter

Collection:
Robert and Beverly Katz, Rome

Exhibited:
American Academy in Rome. "Gregory Gillespie: Quadri Recenti." December 15, 1969-January 7, 1970.

Forum Gallery, New York. "Gregory Gillespie." February 14-March 10, 1970.

The Alpha Gallery, Boston. "Gregory Gillespie: Paintings." April 10-May 1, 1971.

Medici II Gallery, Miami Beach, Florida. "Premiere Exhibition." November 10-30, 1972.

30. Woman on Blue Ground
1969
Mixed media
15½ x 11

Collection:
Forum Gallery, New York

Exhibited:
Forum Gallery, New York.
"Gregory Gillespie." February 14–
March 10, 1970.

Georgia Museum of Art, The
University of Georgia, Athens.
"Gregory Gillespie."
October–November 1970.

The Alpha Gallery, Boston.
"Gregory Gillespie: Paintings."
April 10–May 1, 1971.

Gallery One, Alberta College of
Art, Southern Alberta Institute of
Technology, Calgary.
"Kirschenbaum, Ruhtenberg,
Gillespie." November 1974.

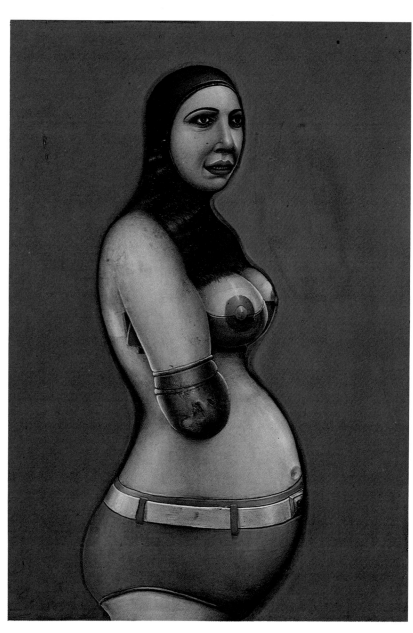

"Actually, this started out as a picture of a movie star."

31. Three Sisters
1969
Oil and magazine photographs
on wood
10¾ x 9¼

Collection:
Mr. and Mrs. Peter B. Ornstein,
New York

Exhibited:
Georgia Museum of Art, The
University of Georgia, Athens.
"Gregory Gillespie."
October–November 1970.

The Alpha Gallery, Boston.
"Gregory Gillespie: Paintings."
April 10–May 1, 1971.

"This picture is a real mix of painted and photographic images. It's in an unfinished state, and I left it like that. It began as a photograph from which I painted out a lot of what was originally in it – I remember a table and other objects. But much of the photograph is left to come through. For instance, the little boy I didn't paint at all. He's really a photograph. So the two painted figures seem real, and the other two seem like ghosts. But psychologically you want them to relate to one another. Everybody has this need to make sense out of things. The mind strains to make sense."

32. Bread Shrine
1969, repainted 1977
Mixed media
47 x 31

Collection:
Dr. and Mrs. Sidney Fierst,
Brooklyn, New York

Exhibited:
Forum Gallery, New York.
"Gregory Gillespie." February 14–
March 10, 1970.

University Gallery, University of
Massachusetts, Amherst.
"Frances Cohen Gillespie and
Gregory Gillespie." September 18-
October 13, 1976.

Rose Art Museum, Brandeis
University, Waltham,
Massachusetts. "From Women's
Eyes." May 1-June 12, 1977.

Reference:
Yard, Sally. Untitled essay. In
From Women's Eyes, edited by Carl
Belz. (Waltham, Massachusetts:
Rose Art Museum, Brandeis
University, 1977), p. 22.

33. Naples Shrine
1969
Mixed media
72 x 48

Collection:
Forum Gallery, New York

Provenance:
Private collection, 1976

Exhibited:
Forum Gallery, New York.
"Gregory Gillespie," February 14–
March 10, 1970.

Forum Gallery, New York.
"Gregory Gillespie: Recent
Paintings." November 13–
December 4, 1976.

Forum Gallery, New York.
"Exhibition of Nine Artists."
July 1-31, 1977.

34. Viva Frances
1969
Mixed media
31 x 27

Collection:
Forum Gallery, New York

Exhibited:
Forum Gallery, New York.
"Gregory Gillespie." February 14–
March 10, 1970.

Georgia Museum of Art, The
University of Georgia, Athens.
"Gregory Gillespie." October–
November 1970.

National Academy of Design,
New York. "146th Annual
Exhibition." February 25–
March 21, 1971. [Receives the
Julius Hallgarten Prize ($350) for
Viva Frances.]

The Alpha Gallery, Boston.
"Gregory Gillespie: Paintings."
April 10–May 1, 1971.

Museum of Art of Ogunquit,
Ogunquit, Maine. "Nineteenth
Annual Exhibition." July 3–
September 6, 1971.

John and Mable Ringling
Museum of Art, Sarasota,
Florida. "After Surrealism:
Metaphors & Similes."
November 17–December 10,
1972.

Gallery One, Alberta College of
Art, Southern Alberta Institute of
Technology, Calgary.
"Kirschenbaum, Ruhtenberg,
Gillespie." November 1974.

35. Roman Landscape (Periphery)
1969
Oil and magazine photographs
on wood
12½ x 16¾

Collection:
Private collection

Exhibited:
Forum Gallery, New York.
"Gregory Gillespie." February 14–
March 10, 1970.

The Alpha Gallery, Boston.
"Gregory Gillespie: Paintings."
April 10–May 1, 1971.

Reference:
Paris, Jeanne. "Art: Gillespie
Prompts a Look Within." *Long
Island Press,* March 8, 1970, p. 31.

36. Self-Portrait (Foro Romano)
1969
Mixed media
25⅜ x 19¾

Collection:
Private collection

Exhibited:
Galleria La Margherita, Rome.
"Estate 1969" ("Summer 1969").
July 3–August 9, 1969.

Forum Gallery, New York.
"Gregory Gillespie." February 14–
March 10, 1970.

37. Cow (Massachusetts)
[also called *Italian Cow Painting*]
1971
Oil and Magna on wood
10 x 12

Collection:
Nathaniel Zimskind

Exhibited:
Smith College Museum of Art,
Smith College, Northampton,
Massachusetts. "Gregory
Gillespie: Recent Paintings."
November 18–December 23, 1971.

Forum Gallery, New York.
"Gregory Gillespie." April 15–
May 5, 1972.

"This was the first painting I did when I came back from Italy. The background is really like the University of Massachusetts, but those trees come out of Italian art. It's really a mixture of things. Some of the elements—like the cinder blocks—you wouldn't see in Italy. It's a blend. I also call this Italian Cow Painting.*"*

38. Early Landscape (Massachusetts)
1971
Oil and Magna on wood
9¾ x 11¾

Collection:
Dr. and Mrs. H. A. T. Bailey, Jr.,
Little Rock, Arkansas

Provenance:
Private collection
Forum Gallery, New York

Exhibited:
Smith College Museum of Art,
Smith College, Northampton,
Massachusetts. "Gregory
Gillespie: Recent Paintings."
November 18–December 23,
1971.

Forum Gallery, New York.
"Gregory Gillespie." April 15–
May 5, 1972.

39. New Hampshire Street Scene
1971
Oil and Magna on wood
12 x 30

Collection:
Mr. and Mrs. Charles K. Wilmers, Geneva

Exhibited:
Smith College Museum of Art, Smith College, Northampton, Massachusetts. "Gregory Gillespie: Recent Paintings." November 18-December 23, 1971.

Forum Gallery, New York. "Gregory Gillespie." April 15-May 5, 1972.

"I wasn't attempting to paint in a different way [from the Italian landscapes] when I did this. I was just trying to capture the local color, which is the same sort of thing I was doing in Italy."

New Hampshire Street Scene

40. Northampton Motor Vehicle Department
1971
Oil and magazine photograph on wood
7 x 9

Collection:
Sydney and Frances Lewis, Richmond, Virginia

Exhibited:
Smith College Museum of Art, Smith College, Northampton, Massachusetts. "Gregory Gillespie: Recent Paintings." November 18-December 23, 1971.

Whitney Museum of American Art, New York. "1972 Annual Exhibition of Contemporary American Painting." January 25-March 19, 1972.

Forum Gallery, New York. "Gregory Gillespie." April 15-May 5, 1972.

References:
Wolmer, Bruce. "Reviews and Previews: Gregory Gillespie." *Art News* 71 (Summer 1972): 19.

"When I went to the Motor Vehicle Department to get my driver's license, they handed out these flyers with photos of Governor Sargent sitting there. They had begun using color photographs on drivers' licenses, and the flyer explained the camera they were using, and so on. This whole scene was actually painted on the flyer they handed out."

41. Hospital
1971
Oil and Magna and magazine
photograph on wood
8 x 7½

Collection:
Helen Searing, Northampton,
Massachusetts

Exhibited:
Smith College Museum of Art,
Smith College, Northampton,
Massachusetts. "Gregory
Gillespie: Recent Paintings."
November 18-December 23, 1971.

Forum Gallery, New York.
"Gregory Gillespie." April 15-
May 5, 1972.

"I had a strange hospital experience, and this painting came out of it. If you've ever had any experience with hospitals, you know it can be a kind of madness. They put me into a category, and gave me stuff I didn't need — one of those Catch-22's. I guess it was those nurses and that clinical setting and the mad leer on their faces, juxtaposed against very rational elements that didn't fit.

"This was painted over a photograph."

42. Plant Life
1971
Oil and Magna on paper
mounted on wood
11½ x 10¼

Collection:
Mr. and Mrs. Jacob M. Kaplan,
New York

Exhibited:
Forum Gallery, New York.
"Gregory Gillespie." April 15–
May 5, 1972.

43. Chinese Landscape with Waterfall
[also called *Chinese Landscape No. 2*]
1971
Oil and Magna on paper
11½ x 10

Collection:
Mr. and Mrs. Philip Horowitz, Long Island City, New York

Exhibited:
Forum Gallery, New York. "Gregory Gillespie." April 15–May 5, 1972.

"I think this was influenced by oriental art, yet in a way it comes out of the landscapes that I did in Italy. It's that same landscape but more bizarre; everything is in a state of transition, of change. You could say these are hallucinatory images with an oriental flavor."

44. The Hall Corner: Graves House
[erroneously called *Interior with Hanging Picture*]
1971
Oil and Magna on Masonite
44½ x 41

Collection:
Permanent Collection of West Virginia University, Morgantown; Gift of Childe Hassam Fund, The American Academy of Arts and Letters, 1972.

Exhibited:
Smith College Museum of Art, Smith College, Northampton, Massachusetts. "Gregory Gillespie: Recent Paintings." November 18–December 23, 1971.

National Academy of Design, New York. "147th Annual Exhibition." February 24–March 19, 1972. [Wins the Saltus Gold Medal for Merit for *The Hall Corner: Graves House*.]

Forum Gallery, New York. "Gregory Gillespie." April 15–May 5, 1972.

The American Academy of Arts and Letters, New York. "Exhibition of Paintings Eligible for Purchase under the Childe Hassam Fund." November 10–December 17, 1972. [*The Hall Corner: Graves House* is purchased

and presented to the Creative Arts Center, West Virginia University, Morgantown.]

References:
Mikotajuk, Andrea. "In the Galleries: Gregory Gillespie." *Arts Magazine* 46 (Summer 1972): 67.

Wolmer, Bruce. "Reviews and Previews: Gregory Gillespie." *Art News* 71 (Summer 1972): 19, 52.

45. Still Life with Grasshopper
1971
Oil and Magna on wood
19¾ x 25

Collection:
Jane Calvin, Santa Monica,
California

Exhibited:
Smith College Museum of Art,
Smith College, Northampton,
Massachusetts. "Gregory
Gillespie: Recent Paintings."
November 18-December 23,
1971.

The Alpha Gallery, Boston.
"Recent Paintings by Gregory
Gillespie." January 5-February 5,
1974.

Forum Gallery, New York.
"Gregory Gillespie — Recent
Work." November 10-30, 1973.

Galleria Il Fante di Spade, Rome.
"Gregory Gillespie: Dipinti
1972-1974." May 30-June 29, 1974
(and tour to Galleria Il Fante di
Spade, Milan, July).

46. Pumice Box and Orange Meditation Piece
1971
Oil and Magna on wood
28 x 33

Collection:
Joseph Feury and Lee Grant, Malibu Beach, California

Exhibited:
Forum Gallery, New York. "Gregory Gillespie." April 15–May 5, 1972.

Reference:
Canaday, John. "Art: In 2 Shows, a Thumbnail Summary." *New York Times,* April 22, 1972, p.29.

47. Self-Portrait (Bald)
1971-72
Mixed media
15 x 10

Collection:
Bella and Sol Fishko, New York

Exhibited:
Forum Gallery, New York.
"Gregory Gillespie." April 15–
May 5, 1972.

48. Farm Scene with Cadillac
1971-72
Oil and Magna on wood
20 x 25

Collection:
Private collection, Italy

Exhibited:
Smith College Museum of Art, Smith College, Northampton, Massachusetts. "Gregory Gillespie: Recent Paintings." November 18-December 23, 1971.

Forum Gallery, New York. "Gregory Gillespie." April 15-May 5, 1972.

The Art Gallery, Randolph-Macon Woman's College, Lynchburg, Virginia. "62nd Annual Exhibition: Contemporary American Painting." February 8-27, 1973.

Galleria Il Fante di Spade, Rome. "Gregory Gillespie: Dipinti 1972-1974." May 30-June 29, 1974 (and tour to Galleria Il Fante di Spade, Milan, July).

References:
Mikotajuk, Andrea. "In the Galleries: Gregory Gillespie." *Arts Magazine* 46 (Summer 1972): 67.

Wolmer, Bruce. "Reviews and Previews: Gregory Gillespie." *Art News* 71 (Summer 1972): 19.

49. Back Entrance: Williamsburg, Massachusetts
1972
Oil and Magna on wood
54 x 84

Collection:
Private collection, Italy

Exhibited:
Forum Gallery, New York, "Gregory Gillespie." April 15–May 5, 1972.

Whitney Museum of American Art, New York. "1973 Biennial Exhibition: Contemporary American Art." Mid-January–mid-March 1973.

Sheldon Memorial Art Gallery, The University of Nebraska — Lincoln. [Exhibited temporarily with permanent collection.] February 1974.

Galleria Il Fante di Spade, Rome. "Gregory Gillespie: Dipinti 1972-1974." May 30–June 29, 1974 (and tour to Galleria Il Fante di Spade, Milan, July).

50. Back Entrance: Post and Stone
[erroneously called *Back Entrance
Corner: Northampton,
Massachusetts*]
c. 1972
Oil and Magna on wood
24 x 35

Collection:
Private collection, Italy

Exhibited:
The New York Cultural Center.
"Realism Now." December 6,
1972-January 7, 1973.

Galleria Il Fante di Spade, Rome.
"Gregory Gillespie: Dipinti
1972-1974." May 30-June 29, 1974
(and tour to Galleria Il Fante di
Spade, Milan, July).

51. Under the Porch
1972-73
Oil and Magna on wood
24 x 35

Collection:
Joseph and Deirdre Garton,
Madison, Wisconsin

Exhibited:
Forum Gallery, New York.
"Gregory Gillespie — Recent
Work." November 10-30, 1973.

The Alpha Gallery, Boston.
"Recent Paintings by Gregory
Gillespie." January 5-February 5,
1974.

Galleria Il Fante di Spade, Rome.
"Gregory Gillespie: Dipinti
1972-1974." May 30-June 29, 1974
(and tour to Galleria Il Fante di
Spade, Milan, July).

52. Garden
1972-73
Oil and Magna and magazine
photograph on wood
8½ x 6½

Collection:
Bella and Sol Fishko, New York

Provenance:
Private collection, 1974

Exhibited:
Forum Gallery, New York.
"Gregory Gillespie — Recent
Work." November 10–30, 1973.

The Alpha Gallery, Boston.
"Recent Paintings by Gregory
Gillespie." January 5–February 5,
1974.

Galleria Il Fante di Spade, Rome.
"Gregory Gillespie: Dipinti
1972–1974." May 30–June 29, 1974
(and tour to Galleria Il Fante di
Spade, Milan, July).

Reference:
Offin, Charles A. "Gallery
Previews in New York: Gregory
Gillespie." *Pictures on Exhibit*
(New York) 37 (December 1973):
16.

53. Woman with Three Dogs
1972-73
Oil and Magna and magazine
photograph on wood
8½ x 8¼

Collection:
Private collection, Italy

Exhibited:
Forum Gallery, New York.
"Gregory Gillespie — Recent
Work." November 10-30, 1973.

The Alpha Gallery, Boston.
"Recent Paintings by Gregory
Gillespie." January 5-February 5,
1974.

Galleria Il Fante di Spade, Rome.
"Gregory Gillespie: Dipinti
1972-1974." May 30-June 29, 1974
(and tour to Galleria Il Fante di
Spade, Milan, July).

54. The Wedding
1972-73
Oil and Magna on wood
17 x 20½

Collection:
Museum of Art, The
Pennsylvania State University,
University Park

Exhibited:
Forum Gallery, New York.
"Gregory Gillespie — Recent
Work." November 10-30, 1973.

The Alpha Gallery, Boston.
"Recent Paintings by Gregory
Gillespie." January 5-February 5,
1974.

Galleria Il Fante di Spade, Rome.
"Gregory Gillespie: Dipinti
1972-1974." May 30-June 29, 1974
(and tour to Galleria Il Fante di
Spade, Milan, July).

Reference:
Offin, Charles Z. "Gallery
Previews in New York: Gregory
Gillespie." *Pictures on Exhibit*
(New York) 37 (December 1973):
16.

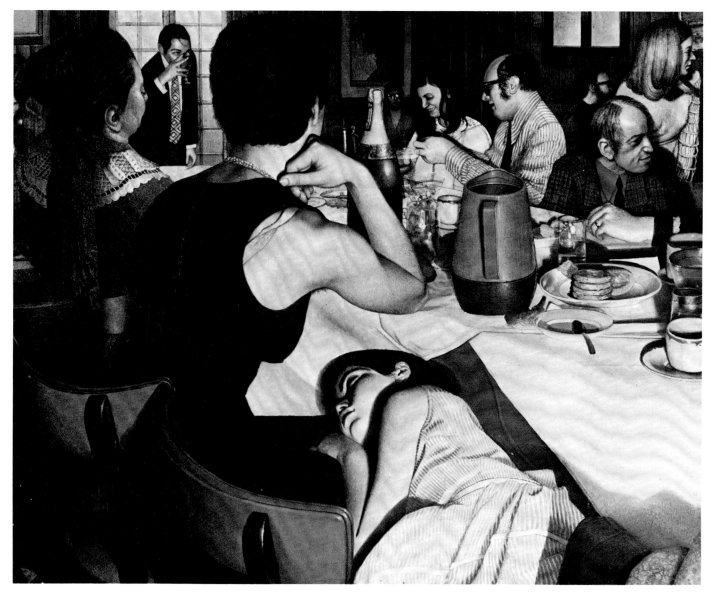

"That was a real wedding; Fran's brother got married and I was the photographer.
I took the slides and turned many of them into color photos because I wanted to do paintings
of them. Then I worked from the print by gridding it. I didn't use to use any mechanical
aids to compose with, but I do now: I had a grid made. I didn't paint on the photograph or
project the slide onto the panel. I copied it from the photograph, very freely."

55. Double Portrait (Fran and Myself)
1973
Oil and Magna on wood
18 x 24

Collection:
George Gilbert, New York

Exhibited:
Forum Gallery, New York. "Gregory Gillespie — Recent Work." November 10-30, 1973.

The Alpha Gallery, Boston. "Recent Paintings by Gregory Gillespie." January 5-February 5, 1974.

Galleria Il Fante di Spade, Rome. "Gregory Gillespie: Dipinti 1972-1974." May 30-June 29, 1974 (and tour to Galleria Il Fante di Spade, Milan, July).

Rose Art Museum, Brandeis University, Waltham, Massachusetts. "From Women's Eyes." May 1-June 12, 1977.

Reference:
Yard, Sally, Untitled essay. In *From Women's Eyes,* edited by Carl Belz. (Waltham, Massachusetts: Rose Art Museum, Brandeis University, 1977), p. 22.

"I copied this from a photograph. If you look closely, you can see a pink flash or glow embedded between them. Sometimes you look at it and it seems like it's the color of the paint on the door, and another time it looks like something else. In the photograph there was a third person, but when I did my painting, I just left her out, and painted the pink glow in — it's sort of embedded in the paint. It's very subtle."

56. Pawn Broker (Porto Portese)
1973
Oil and Magna and magazine
photographs on wood
4¾ x 6¾

Collection:
Private collection, Italy

Exhibited:
Forum Gallery, New York.
"Gregory Gillespie — Recent
Work." November 10-30, 1973.

The Alpha Gallery, Boston.
"Recent Paintings by Gregory
Gillespie." January 5-February 5,
1974.

Galleria Il Fante di Spade, Rome.
"Gregory Gillespie: Dipinti
1972-1974." May 30-June 29, 1974
(and tour to Galleria Il Fante di
Spade, Milan, July).

57. Turtle
1973
Oil and Magna on wood
25 x 27

Collection:
Alfred Ordover, New York

Exhibited:
Forum Gallery, New York.
"Gregory Gillespie — Recent
Work." November 10–30, 1973.

The Alpha Gallery, Boston.
"Recent Paintings by Gregory
Gillespie." January 5–February 5,
1974.

58. Night Vegetation
1973
Oil and Magna on wood
6 x 5½

Collection:
Forum Gallery, New York

Exhibited:
Forum Gallery, New York.
"Gregory Gillespie — Recent
Work." November 10-30, 1973.

The Alpha Gallery, Boston.
"Recent Paintings by Gregory
Gillespie." January 5-February 5,
1974.

Galleria Il Fante di Spade, Rome.
"Gregory Gillespie: Dipinti
1972-1974." May 30-June 29, 1974
(and tour to Galleria Il Fante di
Spade, Milan, July).

Gallery One, Alberta College of
Art, Southern Albert Institute of
Technology, Calgary.
"Kirschenbaum, Ruhtenberg,
Gillespie." November 1974.

The Museum of Modern Art,
New York. "A Museum
Menagerie," Art Lending Service
Penthouse Exhibition. December 9,
1975-March 7, 1976.

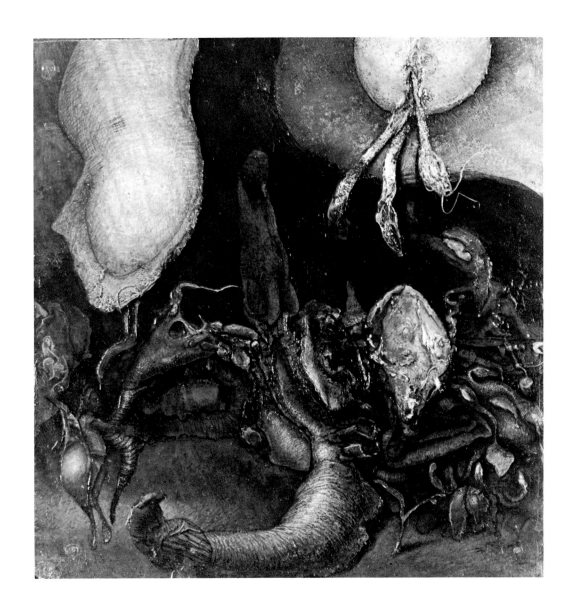

59. Night Garden
1973
Oil and Magna on wood
7½ x 6¾

Collection:
Allan Stone, New York

Exhibited:
Forum Gallery, New York.
"Gregory Gillespie — Recent
Work." November 10-30, 1973.

The Alpha Gallery, Boston.
"Recent Paintings by Gregory
Gillespie." January 5-February 5,
1974.

Galleria Il Fante di Spade, Rome.
"Gregory Gillespie: Dipinti
1972-1974." May 30-June 29, 1974
(and tour to Galleria Il Fante di
Spade, Milan, July).

"Lots of people say Bosch or Breugel when they speak of my work. I've liked them from time to time . . . .I don't know who these kinds of paintings really relate to. Maybe that Victorian Irish painter, Richard Dadd. He was actually insane and he painted little creatures. He's sometimes grouped with the Pre-Raphaelites. He's interesting, this Dadd — he painted the anthropomorphic qualities of nature — goblins, leprechauns."

60. Snake Painting
1973
Oil and Magna on wood
9¾ x 10

Collection:
Mr. and Mrs. Stephen D. Paine, Boston

Exhibited:
Forum Gallery, New York. "Gregory Gillespie — Recent Work." November 10-30, 1973.

The Alpha Gallery, Boston. "Recent Paintings by Gregory Gillespie." January 5-February 5, 1974.

Galleria Il Fante di Spade, Rome. "Gregory Gillespie: Dipinti 1972-1974." May 30-June 29, 1974 (and tour to Galleria Il Fante di Spade, Milan, July).

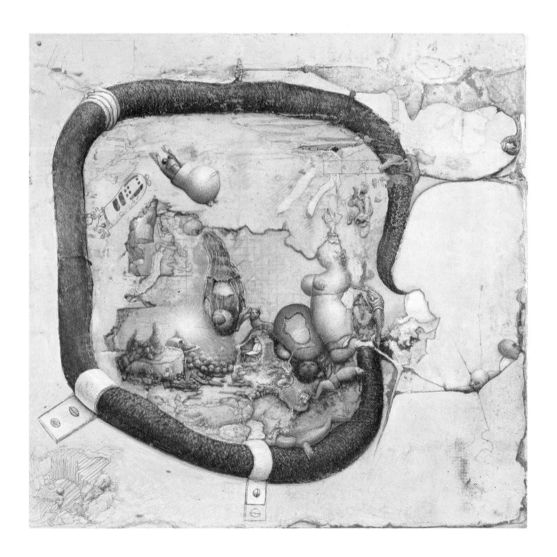

61. Landscape with Horse
[erroneously called *Landscape with House*]
1973
Oil and Magna on wood
9¾ x 11½

Collection:
Nebraska Art Association, Thomas C. Woods Memorial Collection; Courtesy of Sheldon Memorial Art Gallery, University of Nebraska, Lincoln

Exhibited:
Forum Gallery, New York. "Gregory Gillespie — Recent Work." November 10-30, 1973.

The Alpha Gallery, Boston. "Recent Paintings by Gregory Gillespie." January 5-February 5, 1974.

Fogg Art Museum, Harvard University, Cambridge, Massachusetts. [Exhibited temporarily with permanent collection.] Early 1975.

Union Carbide Gallery, New York. "20 American Fulbright Artists," presented by the Institute of International Education. April 3-17, 1975.

Duke University Museum of Art, Durham, North Carolina. [Exhibited during Gillespie's participation in Visiting Artists Program sponsored by the Department of Art and the Undergraduate Teaching Council.] Week of January 26, 1976.

The American Academy of Arts and Letters and The National Institute of Arts and Letters, New York. "Exhibition of Works by Candidates for Art Awards." March 8-April 4, 1976.

The American Academy of Arts and Letters and The National Institute of Arts and Letters, New York. "Exhibition of Work by Newly Elected Members and Recipients of Honors and Awards." May 20-June 13, 1976.

University Gallery, University of Massachusetts, Amherst. "Frances Cohen Gillespie and Gregory Gillespie." September 18-October 13, 1976.

Forum Gallery, New York. "Gregory Gillespie: Recent Paintings." November 13-December 4, 1976.

62. Landscape of the Realm
1973
Oil and Magna on paper
mounted on wood
11½ x 14

Collection:
Graham Gund, Cambridge,
Massachusetts

Exhibited:
The American Academy of Arts
and Letters and The National
Institute of Arts and Letters,
New York. "Exhibition of Work
by Newly Elected Members and
Recipients of Honors and
Awards." May 20-June 13, 1976.

University Gallery, University of
Massachusetts, Amherst.
"Frances Cohen Gillespie and
Gregory Gillespie." September 18-
October 13, 1976.

Forum Gallery, New York.
"Gregory Gillespie: Recent
Paintings." November 13-
December 4, 1976.

Reference:
Betz, Margaret. "New York
Reviews: Gregory Gillespie." *Art
News* 76 (January 1977): 126.

"In fact, this comes off my palette. If the paint on the palette gets interesting, I'll pick it up and paste it down on a panel and start painting into the shapes — 'Rorschaching' into it. It kind of gets involved in a different dimension."

63. Still Life: Studio
1973
Oil and Magna on wood
38 x 34

Collection:
Forum Gallery, New York

Exhibited:
Forum Gallery, New York. "Gregory Gillespie — Recent Work." November 10-30, 1973.

Galleria Il Fante di Spade, Rome. "Gregory Gillespie: Dipinti 1972-1974." May 30-June 29, 1974 (and tour to Galleria Il Fante di Spade, Milan, July).

Union Carbide Gallery, New York. "20 American Fulbright Artists," presented by the Institute of International Education. April 3-17, 1975.

The American Academy of Arts and Letters and The National Institute of Arts and Letters, New York. "Exhibition of Works by Candidates for Art Awards." March 8-April 4, 1976.

The American Academy of Arts and Letters and The National Institute of Arts and Letters, New York. "Exhibition of Work by Newly Elected Members and Recipients of Honors and Awards." May 20-June 13, 1976.

University Gallery, University of Massachusetts, Amherst. "Frances Cohen Gillespie and Gregory Gillespie." September 18-October 13, 1976.

Forum Gallery, New York. "Gregory Gillespie: Recent Paintings." November 13-December 4, 1976.

Rose Art Museum, Brandeis University, Waltham, Massachusetts. "From Women's Eyes." May 1-June 12, 1977.

References:
Brown, Pamela. "Gregory Gillespie." *Arts Magazine* 51 (February 1977): 11.

Yard, Sally. Untitled essay. In *From Women's Eyes,* edited by Carl Belz. (Waltham, Massachusetts: Rose Art Museum, Brandeis University, 1977), pp. 21, 22.

64. Self-Portrait on Bed
1973-74
Oil and Magna on wood
48 x 84

Collection:
Private collection, Italy

Exhibited:
Forum Gallery, New York. "Gregory Gillespie — Recent Work." November 10-30, 1973. [Exhibited in unfinished state.]

The Alpha Gallery, Boston. "Recent Paintings by Gregory Gillespie." January 5-February 5, 1974.

Union Carbide Gallery, New York. "20 American Fulbright Artists," presented by the Institute of International Education. April 3-17, 1975.

The American Academy of Arts and Letters and The National Institute of Arts and Letters, New York. "Exhibition of Work by Newly Elected Members and Recipients of Honors and Awards." May 20-June 13, 1976.

University Gallery, University of Massachusetts, Amherst. "Frances Cohen Gillespie and Gregory Gillespie." September 18-October 13, 1976.

Forum Gallery, New York. "Gregory Gillespie: Recent Paintings." November 13-December 4, 1976.

References:
Betz, Margaret. "New York Reviews: Gregory Gillespie." *Art News* 76 (January 1977): 126.

Brown, Pamela. "Gregory Gillespie." *Arts Magazine* 51 (February 1977): 11.

Gruen, John. "Gregory Gillespie's Dense Reality." *Art News* 76 (March 1977): 79.

65. Visionary Landscape
1974
Oil and Magna on paper
mounted on wood
10 x 8⅜

Collection:
Janet Thomas Swanson,
Cutchogue, New York

66. Self-Portrait (Torso)
1975
Oil and Magna on wood
30¼ x 24¾

Collection:
Sydney and Frances Lewis,
Richmond, Virginia

Exhibited:
The American Academy of Arts
and Letters and The National
Institute of Arts and Letters,
New York. "Exhibition of Works
by Candidates for Art Awards."
March 8– April 4, 1976.

The American Academy of Arts
and Letters and The National
Institute of Arts and Letters,
New York. "Exhibition of Work
by Newly Elected Members and
Recipients of Honors and
Awards." May 20-June 13, 1976.

University Gallery, University of
Massachusetts, Amherst.
"Frances Cohen Gillespie and
Gregory Gillespie." September 18-
October 13, 1976.

Forum Gallery, New York.
"Gregory Gillespie: Recent
Paintings." November 13-
December 4, 1976.

Reference:
Gruen, John. "Gregory
Gillespie's Dense Reality." *Art
News* 76 (March 1977): 78-79.

67. Landscape with Perspective
1975
Oil and Magna on paper
mounted on wood
16¼ x 12¼

Collection:
Sara Roby Foundation
Collection, New York

Exhibited:
Duke University Museum of
Art, Durham, North Carolina.
[Exhibited during Gillespie's
participation in Visiting Artists
Program sponsored by the
Department of Art and the
Undergraduate Teaching
Council.] Week of January 26,
1976.

The American Academy of Arts
and Letters and The National
Institute of Arts and Letters,
New York. "Exhibition of Work
by Newly Elected Members and
Recipients of Honors and
Awards." May 20-June 13, 1976.

University Gallery, University of
Massachusetts, Amherst.
"Frances Cohen Gillespie and
Gregory Gillespie." September 18-
October 13, 1976.

Forum Gallery, New York.
"Gregory Gillespie: Recent
Paintings." November 13-
December 4, 1976.

Reference:
Betz, Margaret. "New York
Reviews: Gregory Gillespie." *Art
News* 76 (January 1977): 126.

68. Red Squash
1975
Oil and Magna on wood
56½ x 45

Collection:
Private collection, Italy

Exhibited:
University Gallery, University of
Massachusetts, Amherst.
"Frances Cohen Gillespie and
Gregory Gillespie." September 18–
October 13, 1976.

Forum Gallery, New York.
"Gregory Gillespie: Recent
Paintings." November 13–
December 4, 1976.

Reference:
Betz, Matgaret. "New York
Reviews: Gregory Gillespie." *Art
News* 76 (January 1977): 126.

69. Still Life with Squash and Rutabagas
1975
Oil and Magna on wood
50 x 41

Collection:
Private collection

Exhibited:
The American Academy of Arts and Letters and The National Institute of Arts and Letters, New York. "Exhibition of Works by Candidates for Art Awards." March 8–April 4, 1976.

The American Academy of Arts and Letters and The National Institute of Arts and Letters, New York. "Exhibition of Work by Newly Elected Members and Recipients of Honors and Awards." May 20–June 13, 1976.

University Gallery, University of Massachusetts, Amherst. "Frances Cohen Gillespie and Gregory Gillespie." September 18–October 13, 1976.

Forum Gallery, New York. "Gregory Gillespie: Recent Paintings." November 13–December 4, 1976.

Rose Art Museum, Brandeis University, Waltham, Massachusetts. "From Women's Eyes." May 1–June 12, 1977.

References:
Betz, Margaret. "New York Reviews: Gregory Gillespie." *Art News* 76 (January 1977): 126.

Yard, Sally. Untitled essay. In *From Women's Eyes,* edited by Carl Belz. (Waltham, Massachusetts: Rose Art Museum, Brandeis University, 1977), p. 22.

70. Studio Wall

[also called *Still Life with Self-Portrait,* in earlier state]
1976
Oil and Magna on wood
96 x 120

Collection:
Forum Gallery, New York

Exhibited:
Forum Gallery, New York. "Gregory Gillespie — Recent Work." November 10-30, 1973. [Exhibited in earlier state.]

The Alpha Gallery, Boston. "Recent Paintings by Gregory Gillespie." January 5-February 5, 1974. [Exhibited in earlier state.]

Forum Gallery, New York. "Gregory Gillespie: Recent Paintings." November 13–December 4, 1976.

Rose Art Museum, Brandeis University, Waltham, Massachusetts. "From Women's Eyes." May 1-June 12, 1977.

References:
Kramer, Hilton. "Art: Drawing from the American Past." *New York Times,* November 26, 1976, sec. C, p. 20.

Brown, Pamela. "Gregory Gillespie." *Arts Magazine* 51 (February 1977): 11.

Yard, Sally. Untitled essay. In *From Women's Eyes,* edited by Carl Belz. (Waltham, Massachusetts: Rose Art Museum, Brandeis University, 1977), pp. 21, 22.

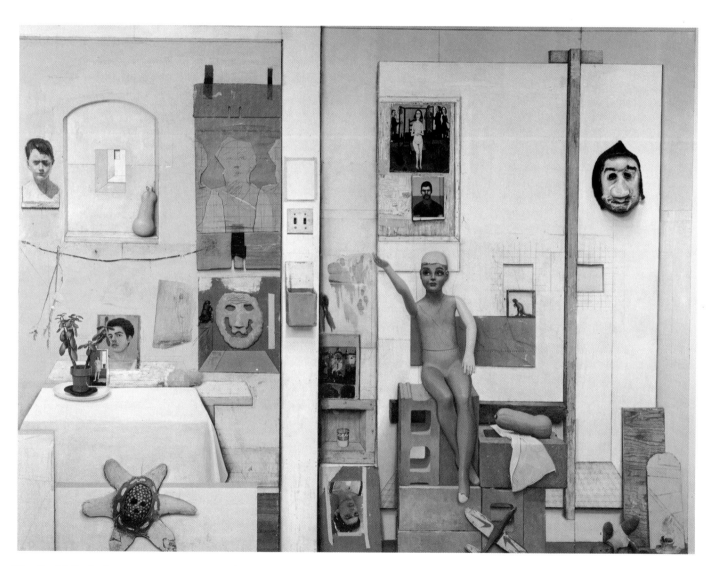

"Studio Wall, *the largest painting I've ever done, really has an evolution. I kept adding panels on to it, and now it's huge, for me. It was around the studio for five years. Twice before I had thought it was finished, and it was exhibited in that original smaller size.*

"*I'd done other wall paintings that were close to* trompe l'oeil *and the notion of fooling the eye; I did my kitchen wall, and a wall in another room just the way it was, mostly with my childrens' things hanging on the wall. So it was a flat surface with relatively simple objects, and it was for the eye. This ten-foot* Studio Wall *evolved from* trompe l'oeil *but got much richer because it came out of the more complex roots of the trattorias and the shrine paintings.*"

71. Landscape with Birch Trees
1976
Oil and Magna on wood
32 x 26

Collection:
Sydney and Frances Lewis,
Richmond, Virginia

Exhibited:
Forum Gallery, New York.
"Gregory Gillespie: Recent
Paintings." November 13–
December 4, 1976.

72. Self-Portrait II
[unfinished]
1976–77
Oil and Magna on wood
32 x 28½

Collection:
Forum Gallery, New York

Exhibited:
University Gallery, University of Massachusetts, Amherst. "Frances Cohen Gillespie and Gregory Gillespie." September 18–October 13, 1976.

Forum Gallery, New York. "Gregory Gillespie: Recent Paintings." November 13–December 4, 1976.

Rose Art Museum, Brandeis University, Waltham, Massachusetts. "From Women's Eyes." May 1–June 12, 1977.

Reference:
Yard, Sally, Untitled essay. In *From Women's Eyes,* edited by Carl Belz. (Waltham, Massachusetts: Rose Art Museum, Brandeis University, 1977), p. 22.

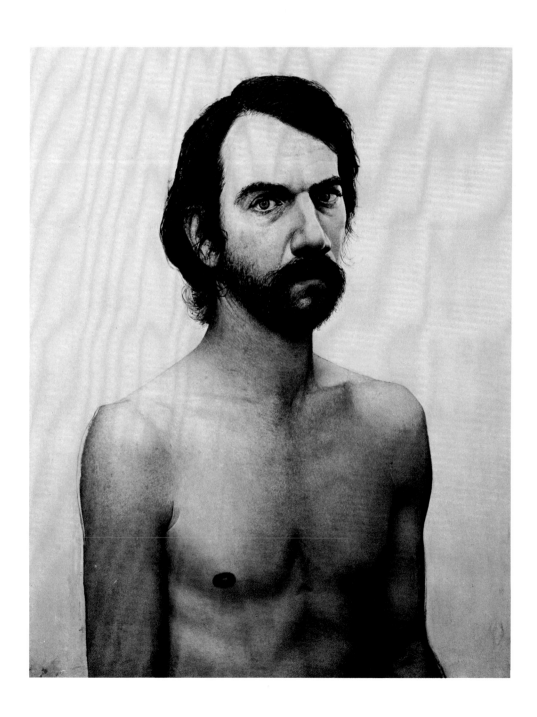

73. Self-Portrait in Studio
1976–77
Oil and Magna on wood
63 x 48

Collection:
Forum Gallery, New York

Chronology	1936	Gregory Joseph Gillespie born November 29, Roselle Park, New Jersey.
	1953	Graduates from Roselle Park High School.
	1954	Enrolls in evening classes at The Cooper Union for the Advancement of Science and Art, New York; later becomes a full-time day student in a nondegree program.
	1959	Marries Frances Cohen, January 25.
	1960	Terminates studies at The Cooper Union; moves to San Francisco to enroll in the degree-granting program in painting at the San Francisco Art Institute.
	1961	Son Vincent born, September 27.
	1962	Graduates from the San Francisco Art Institute, earning both bachelor of arts and master of fine arts degrees, June.
		Is awarded Fulbright-Hays Full Grant; goes to Italy to study Masaccio; lives in the countryside near Florence.
	1963	Daughter Lydia born, May 24.
		Fulbright-Hays Grant renewed for a second year.
	1964	Receives Richard and Hinda Rosenthal Foundation Award ($2,000) "to a younger painter who has not yet been accorded due recognition," in group exhibition at The National Institute of Arts and Letters, New York; uses prize money to travel through Europe.
		Lives in Spain for several months.
		Is awarded Chester Dale Fellowship to study painting at the American Academy in Rome; moves to Rome.
	1965	*Landscape with Mother and Child* is selected for Childe Hassam Fund Purchase, in group exhibition at The American Academy of Arts and Letters, New York.
		Chester Dale Fellowship renewed for a second year.
	1966	Has first one-man exhibition, Forum Gallery, New York.
		Chester Dale Fellowship renewed for a third year.
	1967	Wins gold medal (Medaglia d'Oro della Senato della Repubblica) for *Roman Interior (Still Life)*, in competition of figurative painting involving impressions of Rome.
		Is awarded Louis Comfort Tiffany Foundation Grant for painting ($2,000).
	1969	Has first one-man exhibition in Italy, American Academy in Rome.
	1970	Returns to the United States; lives in Massachusetts.
		Doll-Child is selected for Childe Hassam Fund Purchase, in group exhibition at The American Academy of Arts and Letters, New York.
	1971	Receives the Julius Hallgarten Prize ($350) for *Viva Frances,* in group exhibition at the National Academy of Design, New York.

1972   Wins the Saltus Gold Medal for Merit for *The Hall Corner: Graves House,* in group exhibition at the National Academy of Design, New York.

      The Hall Corner: Graves House is selected for Childe Hassam Fund Purchase, in group exhibition at The National Academy of Arts and Letters, New York.

1976   With Frances Gillespie, teaches informally in Visiting Artists Program at Duke University, Durham, North Carolina, week of January 26; sponsored by the Department of Art and the Undergraduate Teaching Council; three paintings exhibited.

      Receives Academy-Institute Award in Art ($3,000) in group exhibition at The American Academy of Arts and Letters and The National Institute of Arts and Letters, New York.

List of Exhibitions   * indicates one-man exhibition.

1961   THE OAKLAND MUSEUM, OAKLAND, CALIFORNIA. "1961 Northern California Painters' Annual."

      BOLLES GALLERY, SAN FRANCISCO. Group show. December.

      THE AMERICAN ACADEMY OF ARTS AND LETTERS AND THE NATIONAL INSTITUTE OF ARTS AND LETTERS, NEW YORK. "Exhibition of Work by Newly Elected Members and Recipients of Honors and Awards." May 20-August 30. (12 works. Checklist.)

1964   THE NATIONAL INSTITUTE OF ARTS AND LETTERS, NEW YORK. "An Exhibition of Contemporary Painting, Sculpture and Graphic Art." March 13-29. (8 works. Checklist.) Gillespie receives Richard and Hinda Rosenthal Award ($2,000) "to a younger painter who has not yet been accorded due recognition."

1965   THE AMERICAN ACADEMY OF ARTS AND LETTERS, NEW YORK. "Exhibition of Paintings Eligible for Purchase under the Childe Hassam Fund." February 5-21. (1 work. Checklist.) *Landscape with Mother and Child* is purchased and presented to the Riverside Museum, New York, now merged with the Rose Art Museum, Brandeis University, Waltham, Massachusetts.

      AMERICAN ACADEMY IN ROME. "Annual Exhibition of Painting, Sculpture and Architecture." Spring. (1 work. Catalogue: biog., ill.)

      GALLERIA CAPRICORNA, SPOLETO. Group show. Summer. [?]

      GALLERIA FELTRINELLI, ROME. "13 pittore ospiti di Roma" ("13 Painters Sojourning in Rome"). July. [?]

      WHITNEY MUSEUM OF AMERICAN ART, NEW YORK. "1965 Annual Exhibition of Contemporary American Painting." December 8-January 30, 1966. (1 work. Catalogue.)

1966   *FORUM GALLERY, NEW YORK. "Gregory Gillespie: First One Man Exhibition." February 15-26. (20 works. Checklist: biog., ill.)

      GALLERIA DUE MONDE, ROME. "Immagini degli anni '60: poesia e verità" ("Images of the '60s: Poetry and Truth"). February 26-March. (1 work. Catalogue: preface by Duilio Morosini, biog., ill., statement: "I want to be able to paint (reproduce) any object (image) that I chose [sic] to. This is technical. The more difficult problems are the organizations of two or more objects into complex relationships [sic].")

      AMERICAN ACADEMY IN ROME. "Annual Exhibition of Painting, Sculpture and Architecture." Spring. (1 work. Catalogue: biog., ill.)

FLINT INSTITUTE OF ARTS, FLINT, MICHIGAN. "Realism Revisited: Fifty Years of American Realistic Painting Since the Armory Show." April 28-May 29. (1 work. Catalogue: foreword by G. Stuart Hodge.)

1967 GALLERIA IL CAPITELLO, ROME. "1° Premio Internazionale di Pittura Figurativa 'Richiamo di Roma'" ("First International Competition of Figurative Painting 'Recollections of Rome'"). February 18-March 4. (1 work. Catalogue: biog., ill.) Gillespie wins Medaglia d'Oro della Senato della Repubblica (Gold Medal of the Italian Senate) for *Roman Interior (Still Life)*.

THE BUTLER INSTITUTE OF AMERICAN ART, YOUNGSTOWN, OHIO. "32nd Annual Midyear Show." July 2-September 4. (1 work. Catalogue.)

WHITNEY MUSEUM OF AMERICAN ART, NEW YORK. "1967 Annual Exhibition of Contemporary American Painting." December 13-February 4, 1968. (1 work. Catalogue: ill.)

1968 ★FORUM GALLERY, NEW YORK. "Gregory Gillespie." January 9-26. (23 works. Catalogue: foreword by Bella Fishko, biog., ill.)

WHITNEY MUSEUM OF AMERICAN ART, NEW YORK. "Recent Acquisitions." May 23-July 7. (2 works.)

1969 GALLERIA LA MARGHERITA, ROME. "Estate 1969" ("Summer 1969"). July 3-August 9. (3 works. Catalogue: introduction by Sandra Giannattasio, biog., ill.)

GRAHAM GALLERY, NEW YORK. "Artists Abroad," presented by the American Federation of Arts, New York, in cooperation with the Institute of International Education. September 16-December 28, 1971 (touring exhibition). (1 work. Catalogue: biog., ill.)

WHITNEY MUSEUM OF AMERICAN ART, NEW YORK. "Human Concern/Personal Torment: The Grotesque in American Art." October 14-November 30 (and tour to University Art Museum, University of California, Berkeley, January 20, 1970-March 1). (2 works. Catalogue: introduction by Robery Doty, col. ill.)

THE AMERICAN ACADEMY OF ARTS AND LETTERS, NEW YORK. "Exhibition of Paintings Eligible for Purchase under the Childe Hassam Fund." November 14-December 23. (1 work: Checklist.)

★AMERICAN ACADEMY IN ROME. "Gregory Gillespie: Quadri Recenti" ("Gregory Gillespie: Recent Paintings"). December 15-January 7, 1970.

1970 ★FORUM GALLERY, NEW YORK. "Gregory Gillespie." February 14-March 10. (22 works. Checklist. Note: No catalogue issued; *Gregory Gillespie: Paintings (Italy 1962-1970),* a monograph of fifty-six illustrations, including many colorplates, published by Forum Gallery to coincide with the exhibition.)

WHITNEY MUSEUM OF AMERICAN ART, NEW YORK. "Friends' Acquisitions." May 1-24, 1970. (1 work.)

★GEORGIA MUSEUM OF ART, THE UNIVERSITY OF GEORGIA, ATHENS. "Gregory Gillespie." October-November. (11 works. Checklist.)

THE AMERICAN ACADEMY OF ARTS AND LETTERS, NEW YORK. "Exhibition of Paintings Eligible for Purchase under the Childe Hassam Fund." November 12-December 13. (1 work. Checklist.) *Doll-Child* is purchased and presented to the Georgia Museum of Art, The University of Georgia, Athens.

1971 BIRMINGHAM MUSEUM OF ART, BIRMINGHAM, ALABAMA. "Contemporary Selections 1971." January 24-February 20. (1 work. Catalogue.)

NATIONAL ACADEMY OF DESIGN, NEW YORK. "146th Annual Exhibition." February 23-March 21. (1 work. Catalogue.) Gillespie receives the Julius Hallgarten Prize ($350) for *Viva Frances*.

*The Alpha Gallery, Boston. "Gregory Gillespie: Paintings." April 10-May 1. (17 works. Checklist.)

Museum of Art of Ogunquit, Ogunquit, Maine. "Nineteenth Annual Exhibition." July 3-September 6. (1 work. Catalogue.)

The American Academy of Arts and Letters, New York. "Exhibition of Paintings Eligible for Purchase under the Childe Hassam Fund." November 12-December 12. (1 work. Checklist.)

*Smith College Museum of Art, Smith College, Northampton, Massachusetts. "Gregory Gillespie: Recent Paintings." November 18-December 23. (20 works. Checklist: biog., ill.)

1972   Whitney Museum of Amercan Art, New York. "1972 Annual Exhibition of Contemporary American Painting." January 25-March 19. (1 work. Catalogue: ill.)

National Academy of Design, New York. "147th Annual Exhibition." February 24-March 19. (1 work. Catalogue.) Gillespie wins the Saltus Gold Medal for Merit for *The Hall Corner: Graves House* (exhibited with erroneous title *Interior with Hanging Picture*).

*Forum Gallery, New York. "Gregory Gillespie." April 15-May 5. (23 works. Checklist.)

Museum of Art of Ogunquit, Ogunquit, Maine. "Twentieth Annual Exhibition." July 1- September 4. (1 work. Catalogue.)

The Butler Institute of American Art, Youngstown, Ohio. "36th Annual Midyear Show." July 2-September 4. (1 work. Catalogue.)

Medici II Gallery, Miami Beach, Florida. "Premiere Exhibition." November 10-30. (2 works. Checklist.)

The American Academy of Arts and Letters, New York. "Exhibition of Paintings Eligible for Purchase under the Childe Hassam Fund." November 10-December 17. (1 work. Checklist.) *The Hall Corner: Graves House* is purchased and presented to the Creative Arts Center, West Virginia University, Morgantown.

John and Mable Ringling Museum of Art, Sarasota, Florida. "After Surrealism: Metaphors & Similes." November 17-December 10. (3 works. Catalogue: foreword by Leslie Judd Ahlander, biog., ill.)

The New York Cultural Center, New York. "Realism Now." December 6-January 7, 1973. (1 work. Catalogue: foreword by Mario Amaya.)

1973   Whitney Museum of American Art, New York. "1973 Biennial Exhibition: Contemporary American Art." January 10-March 18. (1 work. Catalogue: ill.)

The Art Gallery, Randolph-Macon Woman's College, Lynchburg, Virginia. "62nd Annual Exhibition: Contemporary American Painting." February 8-27. (1 work. Checklist.)

National Academy of Design, New York. "148th Annual Exhibition." February 24-March 18. (1 work. Catalogue.)

*Forum Gallery, New York. "Gregory Gillespie — Recent Work." November 10-30. (26 works. Checklist.)

1974   *The Alpha Gallery, Boston. "Recent Paintings by Gregory Gillespie." January 5-February 5. (23 works. Checklist.)

Krannert Art Museum, College of Fine and Applied Arts, University of Illinois, Urbana-Champaign. "Contemporary American Painting and Sculpture 1974." March 10-April 21. (1 work. Catalogue: introduction by James R. Shipley and Allen S. Weller, biog., ill.)

*Galleria il Fante di Spade, Rome. "Gregory Gillespie: Dipinti 1972-1974" ("Gregory Gillespie: Paintings 1972-1974"). May 30-June 29 (and tour to Galleria Il Fante di Spade, Milan, July). (20 works. Catalogue: biog., ill. Note: According to shipping records at Forum Gallery, the following works, identified by their catalogue numbers in the present exhibition, were exhibited at Galleria Il Fante di Spade: 45, 48, 49, 50, 51, 52, 53, 54, 55, 56, 58, 60. and 63; the following works not in the present exhibition were also shown: *The Beetle and the Frog, Town Planners, Arrest, Car, Creatures (Hostile), Sisters,* and *Chinese Landscape.* Other works listed or illustrated in the Fante di Spade catalogue were apparently not exhibited.)

Hirshhorn Museum and Sculpture Garden, Washington, D.C. "Inaugural Exhibition." October 4, 1974 - October 16, 1975. (2 works. Catalogue: biog., ill. Note: *Two Men Seated* and *Bathers in a Landscape* substituted for *Exterior Wall with Landscape,* illustrated in catalogue but not exhibited.)

Gallery One, Alberta College of Art, Southern Alberta Institute of Technology, Calgary. "Kirschenbaum, Ruhtenberg, Gillespie." November. (8 works. Checklist.)

1975   Union Carbide Gallery, New York. "20 American Fulbright Artists," presented by the Institute of International Education. April 3-17. (3 works. Checklist. Note: *Landscape with Horse* substituted for *Roman Interior (Still Life),* listed as *Roman Interior* in checklist but not exhibited.)

Arte Fiera Di Bologna (Bologna Art Fair). May. (4 works.)

Marion Koogler McNay Art Institute, San Antonio, Texas. "Collector's Gallery IX." November 7-December 25.

The Museum of Modern Art, New York. "A Museum Menagerie," Art Lending Service Penthouse Exhibition. December 9-March 7, 1976. (1 work. Checklist.)

1976   The American Academy of Arts and Letters and The National Institute of Arts and Letters, New York. "Exhibition of Work by Candidates for Art Awards." March 8-April 4. (5 works. Checklist.) Gillespie receives Academy-Institute Award in Art ($3,000).

The American Academy of Arts and Letters and The National Institute of Arts and Letters, New York. "Exhibition of Work by Newly Elected Members and Recipients of Honors and Awards." May 20-June 13. (8 works. Checklist.)

University Gallery, University of Massachusetts, Amherst. "Frances Cohen Gillespie and Gregory Gillespie." September 18-October 13. (17 works. Checklist.)

*Forum Gallery, New York. "Gregory Gillespie: Recent Paintings." November 13-December 4. (15 works. Checklist.)

1977   Rose Art Museum, Brandeis University, Waltham, Massachusetts. "From Women's Eyes." May 1- June 12. (6 works. Catalogue: essay by Sally Yard, biog., ill.)

Oklahoma Art Center, Oklahoma City. "Manscape: 77." May 6-June 5. (1 work. Catalogue: essay by Franz Schulze, ill. Note: *Town Planners* substituted for *Woman Walking in a Room,* illustrated in catalogue but not exhibited.)

Forum Gallery, New York. "Exhibition of Nine Artists." July 1-31. (1 work. Checklist.)

Bibliography

Note: The arrangement is chronological.
Exhibition catalogues are noted in the List of Exhibitions.

Genauer, Emily.   "Painters as Men of 'Letters.'" *New York Herald Tribune,* May 24, 1964, p. 33.

Fagiolo, Maurizio.   "La porn-art *ovvero* La piccola via della salvezza." *La botte e il violino* (Rome) 2 (September 1965): 56 and unpaginated fold-out with three illustrations.

Gendel, Milton.   "Art News from Italy." *Art News* 64 (September 1965): 48-49, 58-59.

"Park Native Sets One-Man Exhibit." *Elizabeth* (N.J.) *Daily Journal,* February 10, 1966, p. 19.

Canaday, John.   "Who Isn't a Realist, Surrealist, Magic Realist or Miniaturist? Give Up?" *New York Times,* February 26, 1966, p. 21

Gruen, John.   "The Galleries — A Critical Guide: Gregory Gillespie." *New York Herald Tribune,* February 26, 1966, p. 8.

Gruen, John.   "The Sad Repast." *New York Herald Tribune,* March 6, 1966, p. 26.

Benedikt, Michael.   "Reviews and Previews: Gregory Gillespie." *Art News* 65 (April 1966): 16.

Berkson, William.   "In the Galleries: Gregory Gillespie." *Arts Magazine* 40 (April 1966): 67.

"Gillespie, Jova Awarded Prizes." *American Academy in Rome Newsletter,* Autumn-Winter 1967.

"Painting Prize." *Daily American* (Rome), February 23, 1967, p. 2.

"'Rome Recollections' Win for U.S. Painter." *Daily American* (Rome), February 24, 1967, p. 6.

Lucas, John.   "Roman Column: Pedestrians & Poets." *Arts Magazine* 41 (May 1967): 15.

Canaday, John.   "At the Galleries: Gregory Gillespie." *New York Times,* January 13, 1968, p. 27.

Browne, Rosalind.   "Reviews and Previews: Gregory Gillespie." *Art News* 66 (February 1968): 12.

"Images: Gregory Gillespie at Forum." *Arts Magazine* 42 (February 1968): 19.

Willard, Charlotte.   "In the Galleries: Rare and Well Done." *New York Post,* February 3, 1968, p. 46.

"Art: Beyond Nightmare." *Time* 93 (June 13, 1969): 74-77.

Schloss, Edith.   "An American Painter's Intense Reality." *International Herald Tribune* (Paris), December 20-21, 1969, p. 7.

"Le mostre: Gregory Gillespie." *L'Espresso* (Rome), January 18, 1970, p. 30.

Perret, George A.   "In the Galleries: Gregory Gillespie at Forum." *Arts Magazine* 44 (February 1970): 63.

Genauer, Emily.   "Art and the Artist." *New York Post,* February 7, 1970, p. 42.

Gruen, John.   "Galleries & Museums: Gregory Gillespie." *New York Magazine* 3 (February 23, 1970): 58.

J. H. R.   "Gregory Gillespies neue Malereien." *Aufbau* (New York), February 27, 1970, p. 10.

Canaday, John.   "Art: Dissent at the Academy of Design." *New York Times,* February 28, 1970, p. 25. [Includes review of Gillespie exhibition at Forum Gallery.]

McSpadden, John.   "In the Galleries: Gregory Gillespie at Forum." *Arts Magazine* 44 (March 1970): 61.

Nordstrom, Sherry C.   "Reviews and Previews: Gregory Gillespie." *Art News* 69 (March 1970): 14, 16.

"Art in New York: Gregory Gillespie." *Time* (New York edition) 95 (March 2, 1970): NY 1.

Paris, Jeanne. "Art: Gregory Gillespie Prompts a Look Within." *Long Island Press,* March 8, 1970, p. 31.

Psychiatry & Social Science Review 4 (July 14, 1970): front cover. [Reproduction of *Exterior Wall with Landscape*; no text.]

"Gillespie Exhibit Now at the Georgia Museum." *Classic Scene* [magazine supplement to *Athens Banner-Herald and The Daily News*], October 4, 1970, p. 3.

Fishko, Bella. "New York Galleries: Forum." *Arts Magazine* 45 (April 1971): 30-31.

Grillo, Jean Bergantini. "Gregory Gillespie: What Do You Mean, Grotesque?" *The Boston Phoenix,* April 13, 1971, p. 26.

Canaday, John. "Art: In 2 Shows, a Thumbnail Summary." *New York Times,* April 22, 1972, p. 29.

Mikotajuk, Andrea. "In the Galleries: Gregory Gillespie." *Arts Magazine* 46 (Summer 1972): 67.

Wolmer, Bruce. "Reviews and Previews: Gregory Gillespie." *Art News* 71 (Summer 1972): 19, 52.

Canaday, John. "Art: Francis Haden Revisited." *New York Times,* November 17, 1973, p. 31. [Includes review of Gillespie exhibition at Forum Gallery.]

Offin, Charles Z. "Gallery Previews in New York: Gregory Gillespie." *Pictures on Exhibit* (New York) 37 (December 1973): 16.

Schwartz, Barry. *The New Humanism: Art in a Time of Change* (New York: Praeger Publishers, 1974), pp. 65, 67-69, 169, colorplate IV [unpaginated].

Pan. "Chronache d'arte: Gregory Gillespie." *La Settimana a Roma,* June 7, 1974, pp. 16-17.

Schloss, Edith. "Around the Galleries in Paris and Rome: Gregory Gillespie." *International Herald Tribune* (Paris), June 8-9, 1974, p. 9.

G. V. "Arte: Il realismo di Gillespie." *Il Messaggero* (Rome), June 10, 1974.

Berenice. "Settevolante: Notizie inutili." *Paese Sera* (Rome), June 12, 1974.

Pan. "Art News." *This Week in Rome,* June 14, 1974, pp. 14-15. [English language version of June 7 entry for Pan.]

Berenice. "Settevolante: Tante scuse a Gillespie, Tornello ecc." *Paese Sera* (Rome), June 18, 1974.

Venturoli, Marcello. "Umberto Mastroianni: i suoi 'sbagli' sono virtù dell'estro." *Il Globo* (Rome), June 23, 1974. [Includes review of Gillespie exhibition at Galleria Il Fante di Spade.]

da Mi. "Mostre a Roma: America intima di Gregory Gillespie." *L'Unità* (Rome), June 26, 1974.

Morosini, Duilio. "Gregory Gillespie: vecchia America." *Paese Sera* (Rome), June 29, 1974.

Da Via', Gualtiero. "Mostreromane: Gillespie al Fante di Spade." *L'Osservatore Romano* (Vatican City), July 4, 1974.

Bonifati, Gaetano Maria. "Le mostre: Alla Galleria 'Il Fante di Spada [sic]'." *Italiastampa* (Rome), July 5, 1974.

Villani, Dino. "Nelle gallerie milanesi: Gillespie." *Libertà* (Piacenza), July 25, 1974.

Villani, Dino. "Mostre d'arte a Milano: Gregory Gillespie." *Gazzetta di Mantova* (Mantua), August 2, 1974. [Text same as July 25 entry for Villani.]

Hogg, Carol. "Two City Galleries Feature New York Art." *Calgary* (Alberta) *Herald,* November 8, 1974.

"For the Record." *The Art Gallery* 19 (April/May 1976): 72.

Georgia, Olivia, and Lubov, Sandra J. "Sacred Ships, Flesh and Flora." *Below the Salt* [weekly fine arts supplement to *Daily Collegian* (Amherst, Mass.)], September 30, 1976, pp. 4-5.

Pawlikowski, Betsy. "Redoing Reality." *Valley Advocate* (Amherst, Mass.), October 6, 1976, sec. II, p. 28.

J. H. R. "Gregory Gillespie: Neue Malerien." *Aufbau,* November 19, 1976, p. 11.

Kramer, Hilton. "Art: Drawing from the American Past." *New York Times,* November 26, 1976, sec. C, p. 20. [Includes review of Gillespie exhibition at Forum Gallery.]

Betz, Margaret. "New York Reviews: Gregory Gillespie." *Art News* 76 (January 1977): 126.

Brown, Gordon. "Arts Reviews: Gregory Gillespie." *Arts Magazine 51* (January 1977): 51.

Brown, Pamela. "Gregory Gillespie." *Arts Magazine* 51 (February 1977): 11.

Gruen, John. "Gregory Gillespie's Dense Reality." *Art News* 76 (March 1977): 78-81.

Friedberg, Arleen. "From Woman's [sic] Eyes: Four Young Curators at the Rose Art Museum." *Boston Entertaining Arts* 5 (May 1977): 14-15.

Dyer, Ellen. "Brandeis Show: Contemporary Directions." *Boston Patriot Ledger* (Quincy, Mass.), May 10, 1977, p. 34.

Taylor, Robert. "'Women's Eyes' a Stimulating Exhibit." *Boston Globe,* May 15, 1977. p. A10.

Garrett, Larry. "'Women's Eyes' Seen at Rose Art Museum." *Boston Herald American,* May 22, 1977, sec. 8, pp. 37, 41.

Canaday, John. "Here We Go Again." *The New Republic* 77 (October 1, 1977): 28-29.